www.wadsworth.com

wadsworth.com is the World Wide Web site for Wadsworth Publishing Company and is your direct source to dozens of online resources.

At *wadsworth.com* you can find out about supplements, demonstration software, and student resources. You can also send e-mail to many of our authors and preview new publications and exciting new technologies.

wadsworth.com
Changing the way the world learns®

THINKING
ABOUT
RACE

Naomi Zack
University of Albany
State University of New York

Wadsworth Publishing Company
I(T)P® An International Thomson Publishing Company

Belmont, CA • Albany, NY • Bonn • Boston • Cincinnati • Detroit
Johannesburg • London • Madrid • Melbourne • Mexico City
New York • Paris • Singapore • Tokyo • Toronto • Washington

Philosophy Editor: Peter Adams
Assistant Editor: Kerri Abdinoor
Editorial Assistant: Kelly Bush
Print Buyer: Stacey Weinberger
Production: Matrix Productions
Composition: R&S Book Composition
Copy Editor: Deborah Meyers
Cover Design: Stanton Design
Printer: R.R. Donnelley & Sons/Crawfordsville

Printed in the United States of America
5 6 7 8 9 10

For more information, contact Wadsworth Publishing Company, 10 Davis Drive, Belmont, CA 94002, or electronically at http://www.wadsworth.com/wadsworth.html.

International Thomson Publishing Europe
Berkshire House 168-173
High Holborn
London, WC1V 7AA, England

International Thomson Editores
Campos Eliseos 385, Piso 7
Col. Polanco
11560 México D.F. México

Thomas Nelson Australia
102 Dodds Street
South Melbourne 3205
Victoria, Australia

International Thomson Publishing Asia
221 Henderson Road
#05-10 Henderson Building
Singapore 0315

Nelson Canada
1120 Birchmount Road
Scarborough, Ontario
Canada M1K 5G4

International Thomson Publishing Japan
Hirakawacho Kyowa Building, 3F
2-2-1 Hirakawacho
Chiyoda-ku, Tokyo 102, Japan

International Thomson Publishing GmbH
Königswinterer Strasse 418
53227 Bonn, Germany

International Thomson Publishing
   Southern Africa
Building 18, Constantia Park
240 Old Pretoria Road
Halfway House, 1685 South Africa

Library of Congress Cataloging-in-Publication Data
Zack, Naomi,
      Thinking about race/Naomi Zack.
         p.   cm.
      Includes bibliographical references and index.
      ISBN 0-534-53442-2
      1. Race. 2. Racism. I. Title.
HT1521.Z33   1998
   305.8—dc21   97-32407

To my sons, Alexander Linden Erdmann and Bradford Zack Mahon

"WHEN MICHEL FOUCAULT WAS ASKED WHAT WAS HIS CONCEPTION OF A BOOK, HE REPLIED: A TOOL BOX."

—GILLES DELEUZE AND FELIX GUATTARI

CONTENTS

CHAPTER 4
ETHNICITY   29

CHAPTER 5
RACISM   38

CHAPTER 6
PUBLIC POLICY AND AFFIRMATIVE ACTION   48

CHAPTER 7
WHITENESS   58

CHAPTER 8
RACIAL AND ETHNIC IDENTITY   67

PREFACE AND ACKNOWLEDGMENTS

This book is meant to be a toolbox for thinking rationally and reasonably about race. It is designed for the college classroom but I hope it will also be useful for high school seniors and juniors and anyone else who wants to calmly reflect, talk, and write about the topics and problems concerning race that confront us at the close of the twentieth century in the United States. The conceptual approach might also serve as a warmup or overview for graduate students and other scholars new to the subject matter.

Peter Adams, philosophy and religion editor at Wadsworth, suggested I write a short textbook on race when he stopped at my office during the fall of 1995. By that time I had already written and edited theoretical books and articles about race, and it was a new idea that some of this scholarship could be a foundation for introductory course material. I had designed a course called *Philosophy and Race* for the Department of Philosophy at the University at Albany but had not yet taught it. So my initial reaction to Peter's suggestion was tentative.

During the spring 1996 semester, my *Philosophy and Race* course was scheduled for the following fall. I decided to compile a course reader of reprints, which would be framed by a series of topic analyses. It occurred to me that those analyses could be put together as a book proposal for Wadsworth, and that if the proposal were accepted I could use my lecture notes for the course, as well as my experience in the classroom, to write the book. And that is basically what happened. Wadsworth's external reviewers reacted favorably to the proposal, and the material for the chapters of the book emerged from lectures and class discussions. I told my students that the general idea was to apply philosophical methods of investigation and argument to issues concerning race, and that I intended to learn from their opinions and reflections. My students of PHI 328, *Philosophy and Race,* fall, 1996, helped me understand how to apply basic philosophical tools to race in ways that addressed their present concerns, and I hereby thank them, very warmly, albeit alphabetically: Constance Aker, Cynthia L. Asmus, Eleni D. Athanasiou, Jordan H. Bennett, Michael H. Berendt, Craig A. Bergen, Rachel B. Blatter, Jean-Jacques Cadet, Greg K. Campbell, Hyacinth Chu, Jereme B. Corrado, Jessica M. Costosa, Rebecca A. Curry, Christophe D'Arconte, Charles S. Dixon, Jeremy W. Fibiger, Michael A. Furgang, Joseph A. Gallagher, Mark T. Gorthey, Denis M. Kaye, Kathleen B. Keough, Roland J. Lavigne, Jr., Hwanhee "Mark" Lee, Miamah Jo Richards, Dorey A. Roland, Elizabeth A. Rudolph, Michael C. Schoenbach, Kevin V. Sheehan, Niels Ter Meulen, John P. Urcioli, Frederic K. Vanstrander, Nisse Varghese, Brian M. Vicari, Wendy L. Weidman, and Michael G. Wood.

I have been writing and speaking about many of the subjects addressed in this book since 1991. Faculty and student audience responses to my talks on aspects of the subjects presented in chapters here were an important background contribution as I wrote the manuscript. I am grateful for comments and discussion following my presentations at the University at Albany, Brown University, University of California at Berkeley, Carleton University (Ottawa), Dickenson College, University of Helsinki, Nazareth College, University of Pittsburgh, Rutgers University, Trinity College, Vassar College, and Eastern and Western Division meetings of the American Philosophical Association from 1994 to 1997.

I am very grateful to Laurie Shrage for the care she took in reading the entire prepublication manuscript and in writing comments and suggestions on many, many pages. This close reading for stylistic presentation, scholarship, and conceptual clarity was a supportive and much needed collegial gift, rarely received by academic writers in these times of general overwork. I followed most of her suggestions and the book is better for Laurie being a friend to it, and to me.

I am also grateful to Crispin Sartwell, my valued e-mail friend and colleague, for ongoing discussion about the topics in the book as well as an encouraging reading of Chapter 7.

As always, I have been empowered by the support of my colleagues in the Department of Philosophy at the University at Albany, especially Bob Howell, who while he was Chair expressed his goodwill, and that of other members of the Department, toward me in ways too numerous to document. Thanks, also, in particular, to Tony Ungar for confirming the contradictory logical structure of black and white racial categories, as discussed in Chapter 1.

Wadsworth's four external anonymous reviewers of the penultimate manuscript provided much detailed constructive criticism and suggestions for fine-tuning. The final work is more clear and comprehensive than it would have been without their influence on the last revision. Their comments from feminist, legal, critical thinking, and African American philosophy perspectives led to additional bibliographic sources, additions to the glossary, qualifications in some places, wider claims in others, and altogether more precision.

Thanks also to Merrill Peterson and Terri Froemel at Matrix Productions for getting the manuscript to press. Deborah Meyers made sure that the glossary was complete and references were accurate during copyediting.

My friend Helena Jia Hershel provided ongoing e-mail encouragement and company which made the project much easier to complete on a daily basis.

I want to express appreciation to my older son, Alex, who was always positive about the project during our telephone conversations. Alex and I have had many informative and reinforcing discussions about race over the past five or six years. He is an artist and a writer, now studying film at U.C.L.A., who has lived through many problems concerning racial identity and racism while growing up in Los Angeles.

I am deeply indebted to my younger son, Bradford, who made time out of an overwhelming junior year schedule as a student at the Albany Academy to read and offer suggestions on the penultimate copy of the manuscript. Bradford and I are mutually unsparing when it comes to criticism so when something has his stamp of approval, I know it's okay.

My students and my sons are part of the generation that will have well-formed memories of the twentieth century as they reach full adulthood in the twenty-first. W. E. B. Du Bois' prediction that the main American social problem in the twentieth century would involve race has proved true. It may also hold for the twenty-first century. But it will not hold for the next millennium. This generation of my sons and students is destined to span two millennia. They have the right stuff to do that: speed, strength, skill, talent, ambition, and desire for all of the good things this earth still has to offer. The complaint of some members of my generation that they are not humanitarians and scholars obscures the ease with which these young adults learn what they need to know. As they come into their full powers, their compassion will flower. Some of them will love truth or beauty for its own sake. They will honor us.

A book like this emerges through a social process, as mention of the contributions above indicates. Still, I know it has flaws, gaps, blind spots—those are mine.

Naomi Zack
Albany, NY
October, 1997

INTRODUCTION

A. TO THE INSTRUCTOR

This book develops conceptual tools for addressing race in American life and scholarship. It can be used by itself or supplemented with further readings from sources selected by the instructor, chosen by the student, or recommended here. The general ideas presented arise out of and are inspired by the vast, multidisciplinary, existing literature on race. For this reason, footnotes keyed into the text would be arbitrary and distracting to the flow of thought the reader is invited to develop. The aim is to enable a forum in which ideas about race are addressed analytically and critically, with dialogue, emphasis, and content provided by the particular thinking context. The general context assumed for this forum is the United States at the close of the twentieth century, though many of the issues may apply to other cultural and national situations.

B. TO THE STUDENT

Background

During the 1980s and 1990s, many Americans have come to see themselves as "a society divided by race." There are complex political, economic, and social reasons for this image, even though racial divisions are accepted as a natural part of everyday life. The causes of many of these divisions can be found in recent historical changes. American demographics of race, as recorded in the U.S. census, changed dramatically between 1950 and 1990: the percent of the population listed as *white*[1] decreased from 89 percent to 80 percent; the percent listed as *black* increased from 11 percent to 12 percent; *Native Americans,* Eskimos, and Aleut increased to 1 percent; the category of *"other"* increased from 1 percent to 4 percent; Asian Americans have increased in population from about 1 million to 7 million; 9 percent of Americans were listed as Hispanic (an ethnic category that overlapped with the racial categories). Also between 1950 and 1990, the percentage of women in the workforce increased from 27 to 45, and 70 percent of women ages 25–64 were employed outside the home in 1990.

A politically significant part of the white middle class has recently returned to *traditional values* that are not shared by all members of a racially *pluralistic society.* The U.S. economy has stopped expanding, resulting in more competition for desirable

---

[1]See glossary for words and phrases in *boldface italic.*

jobs and educational opportunities. Fiscal *conservatism* in government has led to budget cuts in human services, public education, and other forms of institutional assistance to minority racial groups, women, and the poor. There is an increased awareness of racial differences because most people of color now affirm their distinct racial identities as positive aspects of themselves and their culture; and, many whites are coming in contact with people of color for the first time in schools and workplaces, due to integration resulting from the civil rights movements.

The ways in which the United States is divided by race vary according to the race and politics of those concerned. Thus, a difference in race may result in a difference in *perspective* or point of view on racial problems. Examples of contemporary racial divisions include the following. African Americans are disproportionately poor, unemployed, and "in" the criminal justice system. Middle-class African Americans do not think that their positions are secure or that whites fully recognize their achievements. *Neoconservative* intellectuals and academics are claiming that poor African Americans are the cause of their own problems, either because they are born with lower intelligence or do not value family and work the same way the white majority does. Many Hispanic and Asian immigrants are employed at subsistence wages in industry and agriculture. Native Americans claim that their culture, as well as their land, has been appropriated by the white majority. Many whites believe that *affirmative action* is a form of *reverse discrimination* that unjustly deprives them of opportunities for education and employment. American social life and housing remain segregated by race, and new forms of apparently voluntary segregation have developed in places that were once assumed would be models of integration, such as college campuses. Many parents, students, teachers, and college professors insist that educational curricula are biased against nonwhites because they perpetuate intellectual traditions that have always been dominated by white men. Others with a stake in the educational system claim that *multiculturalism* undermines standards that must be met for anyone to get an education. Participants in a *mixed-race* movement are demanding recognition in new racial categories. An old ideology of *white supremacy* seems to have taken on new life on the fringes of society, and racial hate crimes appear to be on the rise, even in the military. A new area of scholarship called *whiteness studies* addresses whiteness as an identity that people create, while a tongue-in-cheek backlash affirms *white-trash* identities. And so on.

Aims of This Book

Perhaps Americans are not so much divided by race as splintered by it. Certainly, race is a topic that few are able to discuss in depth without strong feelings of frustration and anger. The first job of this book is to introduce some neutral concepts to racial topics to assist the student in *thinking critically* about race. Thinking critically about race is the same as thinking critically about any other topic. One uses *basic rules of logic* and requires *good evidence* for factual claims. These rules of *logic* largely mirror ordinary intuitions about whether conclusions are justified. Their use in critical thinking does not require formal training but simply an avoidance of contradiction and an awareness of when one statement "follows" from another. In constructing logical arguments or making a persuasive case for an opinion, all of the gaps in reasoning ought to be filled in.

What counts as good evidence for factual claims is often a matter of common-sense. Scientific claims that have withstood examination and duplication by other scientists, or commonsense claims that are supported by a wide range of ordinary experience, are examples of good evidence. Speculations, personal opinions, emotional reactions, and generalizations drawn from a few examples are not good evidence for claims made about racial groups—or about anything else.

Because race is often an emotionally charged subject, learning to think critically about race is difficult. But once the difficulties have been faced, the same critical thinking skills can be applied to other subjects. All critical thinking skills are learned and developed through thinking, reading, writing, and conversation.

While thinking critically about race does not directly solve racial problems, it can enlarge the area in which people agree to disagree in orderly ways. Of course, race is more than an academic subject. Race is an important part of personal and public daily life. The second job of this book is to encourage the student to bring his or her own racial experience to bear on the academic subject of race. Some will want to share their particular experience in discussion and writing, while others will want to retain their privacy. Both choices deserve the same degree of respect.

The combination of thinking critically about race as an academic subject, and relating one's own experience to that work, should result in greater understanding of treatments of race in the news media, popular culture, and art. It should also make it easier to understand the opinions of those with different experiences of race. Personal attitudes and opinions may also change in ways that are difficult to predict. Therefore, the third job of this book is to assist the student in developing ***principles,*** or general moral rules for behavior, and ***strategies,*** or ways of achieving goals, for dealing with race in daily life.

Structure of the Book

The book is divided into eleven chapters and a conclusion that represent areas of current scholarly and practical concern about race. At the top of each chapter is a thought exercise. The chapters progress cumulatively and discussions in later chapters rely on earlier analyses. Each chapter begins with an introduction and overview of the topics covered. Then the topics are ***analyzed,*** that is, they are broken down into their simplest concepts and those concepts are related to one another. The chapters conclude with questions for discussion, reflection, and essay writing, and recommendations for further reading. The recommended readings are meant to provide content for the issues raised in the chapter sections, but the reader is also expected to find and apply additional or alternative material from other study and life experience. There is a vast array of scholarly publication about race in philosophy, history, literature, sociology, psychology, anthropology, feminism, fields of specific racial and ethnic studies, and other sources including print media, theater, art, movies, music, and popular fiction. It is hoped that the tools developed while working with this book will help the reader sort out the parts of that material that interest him or her.

A Personal Note

As your author, I feel I should disclose to you now that I am a philosopher, a woman, and a mixed-race American, probably in that order. While I've tried to present the aspects of race that lend themselves to critical thinking with as much ordinary logic and good evidence as I can muster, the reader should rely on his or her own careful judgment and be encouraged to disagree with the text as necessary.

Because black-white race relations and black *liberation* have been the most problematic aspects of race in American history, there is often more in this book about African American perspectives than about white, Asian, or Native American. However, a strong attempt has been made to address American racial differences broadly and inclusively. If students feel that their racial or ethnic group and its unique problems have not been satisfactorily represented, it is hoped that they will make their views known in class discussion. I also hope that such underrepresented students will take the time to write to me so that I can take your concerns into account in future editions.

Prof. Naomi Zack
Philosophy Department
HU 257
University at Albany, SUNY
Albany, NY 12222
e-mail: nzack@cnsunix.albany.edu

C. DISCUSSION QUESTIONS

1. Make as long a list as you can of additional current problems with race.

2. Choose one or two positions on race and state why you agree with them, or else argue against them.

3. Describe the last time you felt angry or frustrated about a racial issue. Explain what you were thinking and what you think the other party was thinking.

4. Describe several ordinary rules of logic that are important for thoughtful discussion. Explain how they apply to discussions about racial issues.

5. Give examples of good evidence in several racial contexts.

D. RECOMMENDED READING[2]

Statistical information on race can be found in U.S. Bureau of the Census, *Characteristics of the Population,* 1970; and in U.S. Bureau of the Census, *Census of Population: General Population Characteristics—United States,* 1990. Cornel West, in

---

[2]Sources listed in the *Recommended Reading* sections of chapters are fully cited in the bibliography at the end of the book.

Race Matters, considers black-white racial divisions from the position of being black. Contemporary philosophers discuss the situations of poor urban blacks in Bill E. Lawson, ed., *The Underclass Question.* Dinesh D'Souza argues that American black cultural values are the source of black problems in *The End of Racism.* In *Blood in the Face,* James Ridgeway chronicles recent white supremacist ideology. For analysis of racial whiteness as a social and political identity, see Michael Omi and Howard Winant, *Racial Formation in the United States: From the 1960's to the 1980's.* The debate about affirmative action is closely analyzed by Gertrude Ezorsky in *Racism and Justice.* M. A. Jaimes, ed., presents a range of Native American political positions in *The State of Native America.* Problems faced by contemporary Asian Americans are described and discussed in separate contributions from Karen Hossfeld, Bonnie Thornton Dill, and Nazli Kibria in Maxine Baca Zinn and Bonnie Thornton Dill, eds., *Women of Color in U.S. Society.* Issues of American mixed-race identities are explored in Naomi Zack, ed., *American Mixed Race: The Culture of Microdiversity.* The basic rules of logic and the importance of evidence in critical thinking can be found in introductory logic textbooks, such as Irving M. Copi's *Introduction to Logic,* as well as in textbooks on informal logic, such as *Understanding Arguments* by Robert J. Fogelin.

Y OU ARE A COLLEGE FRESHMAN ASSIGNED TO A DORM. WHEN
YOU MEET YOUR ROOMMATE FOR THE FIRST TIME, THERE IS A
HALF-SECOND PAUSE BEFORE YOU INTRODUCE YOURSELVES. IN THAT
HALF-SECOND, EACH OF YOU HAS PERCEIVED THAT THE OTHER IS A
DIFFERENT RACE. HOW DID YOU EACH KNOW THAT? WHAT DOES IT
MEAN TO SAY THAT SOMEONE BELONGS TO THIS OR THAT RACE?

CHAPTER 1

WHAT IS RACE?

INTRODUCTION

We take *race* for granted in the United States, and someone's race may be the first
thing you notice about a person you do not know. We acknowledge that there are serious "racial tensions" and "racial problems" in our society. If pressed, what most of
us understand by those expressions is that people of different races react to one another with hostility because they are of different races, and that members of each
race have problems that are the result of being members of their race. We do not
usually think that there is anything wrong with the ways in which people are sorted
into races—that is, with the *criteria* for membership in different races—because we
think that what race a person belongs to is obvious from looking at him or her. We
do not question the *naturalness* of racial differences or the very existence of races.
We go on about our business as though there always have been human races and
there always will be human races. We assume that the physical differences that make
up the different races have always been the same and always been thought about in
the same ways.

In fact, the word *race* and the idea the word stands for have meant very different things throughout Western European and American history. Section A is an
analysis of some of those different historical meanings. The core meaning of race at
present would seem to be distinctive biological types of human beings that can be
studied by scientists. This suggests that scientists must have an idea of race that could
give our ordinary thinking about racial difference some stability. But the biological
sciences do not have useful or verified concepts of race at this time and there is no
reason to believe that they ever will. In Section B, the problems with race in the biological sciences are analyzed. Despite the lack of a physical, scientific foundation,
categories of race remain deeply embedded in common sense and social reality. Section C analyzes the definitions of black, white, Indian, and Asian race that have been
in use in American society since about 1900, and then offers some observations
about broad cultural ideas of race.

1

A. THE HISTORY OF THE CONCEPT OF RACE

A *word* is a sign or sound that stands for something else, usually a thing that exists outside of the mind, an image in the mind, or a *concept.* A concept is an idea or the meaning of a word. Concepts change over time and these changes depend on the historical situations in which they are used. Words may be spelled and pronounced the same from one century to the next, or they may look and sound different. In both cases, the same concepts can sometimes be traced. In translations between different languages, a word may look and sound the same and stand for a different concept, or look and sound different but stand for the same concept. Throughout European history, until the eighteenth and nineteenth centuries, the word *race* (and its synonyms and the words for it in different languages) meant family or national group. In ancient Greece and Rome, a person's race was the group to which he or she belonged, associated with an ancestral place and culture. During the Middle Ages, a person's race was literally his or her family and ancestors, in the sense of a *line,* which was an English synonym for race. By the seventeenth century, the start of the modern period in which nation-states began to emerge, the word race was associated with cultures and civilizations in particular geographic areas. Through the eighteenth century, while physical differences such as the darker skin hues of Africans were associated with race, racial divisions were based on differences in religion and cultural tradition rather than on human biology. Indeed, the modern science of biology, with systematic methods for dividing living things into genus, species, and subspecies, was not developed until the late eighteenth and early nineteenth centuries. Ancestry, culture, biology: each of these was a different historical concept of race.

By the second half of the nineteenth century all the earlier concepts were combined, and *race* came to mean a distinct biological group of human beings who were not all members of the same family but who shared inherited physical and cultural traits that were different from those shared within other races. This meaning of race was constructed by American scientists during slavery and segregation. The claims of these scientists of race were used as justifications for black chattel slavery and white social and economic dominance over Negroes. Based on reports of *empirical* findings that were often incomplete or even falsified, hierarchies of human races were postulated. Always, the black race was on the bottom and the white race on the top, with Asians and Indians in the middle. Nineteenth-century racial theory posited inherited *racial essences* as the cause of superior or inferior intellectual, aesthetic, spiritual, and moral qualities. This concept of race was more *abstract* than the older family line concept, because it posited race as the cause of characteristics that were inherited through family descent. It was also more *general* because each of the main racial groups included many family lines within them. The notion of essence did not allow for mixed essences; in cases of racial mixture it was assumed that offspring inherited the essence of the hierarchically "inferior" race. During the early twentieth century, social scientists began to realize that differences in human culture, behavior, intellect, morality, and spirituality were the result of environment, education, and history rather than biology. As a result, the concept of race shrank to mean biological differences only. That is, at present, as a factual basis for individual and group identification, "race" still means inheritable physical characteristics only.

B. THE PROBLEMS WITH RACE IN SCIENCE

If you ask adult Americans what race is, you might be told that races are different *breeds* of human beings and that the elementary school books used to say that there were three of them: Negro, Caucasian, and Mongoloid, or in current language, black, white, and Asian. The U.S. census and most public institutions gather information and keep records based on the racial categories of black, white, Asian or Pacific Islander, and American Indian or Alaska Native. In recent decades, everyone who has been a student or an employee, or filled out an application to participate in a large public institution has been required to indicate what their race is at some stage in complying with requests for information. As well as information on race, *Hispanic* or non-Hispanic *ethnicity* has to be indicated.

The Hispanic category was artificially created by the U.S. government and it contains wide racial variation. Some members of the group whom the government considers Hispanic claim that they should be identified as *Latino[/a]* or *Chicano[/a]*. People who are *biracial* or *multiracial* are often frustrated by the bureaucratic system of racial classification that these forms represent because they are usually asked to designate themselves by one race only. Their only alternative to this is to *identify* as *"other"*.

Still, most Americans believe that the information requested on such forms has a factual basis apart from its interest to officials. The 1990 U.S. census recorded the following data for a population of 249 million: 200 million whites; 30 million blacks; 7 million Asians and Pacific Islanders; 2 million Native Americans, Eskimos, and Aleut; 10 million who were "other." Additionally, there were 22 million Hispanics. The presumption that these figures mean something is very strong. They are taken seriously as a basis for *entitlement* programs for nonwhite minority groups, and used for information about the population by business and educational institutions. They are also a source for national, group, and individual self-images. Individuals believe that their types of skin color, hair texture, facial features, and bone structure are the results of belonging to the race to which they belong. And the race to which you belong, even if it is that cryptic category of "other," has a place on the national map of races.

If it were true that being black, white, Asian, or Indian caused human beings to have the types of physical traits they do, then there ought to be some physical marker for race, apart from those traits, that scientists can identify. Otherwise, there would be nothing general about a race that could cause distinctive types of physical traits in individuals. However, neither biologists, nor anthropologists, nor physiologists, nor geneticists, nor any of the other scientists who have studied physical race have ever identified any general racial characteristics shared by all members of any particular race. There are no genes or other hereditary factors shared by every member of any of the main racial groups. In this sense, race provides an interesting contrast to biological sex. There are chromosomal markers of XY and XX, respectively, for male and female biological sex. Given the presence of XY or XX, the presence of more specific sexual traits, such as testicles or ovaries, can be predicted. But there is nothing analogous for race. When scientists study physical traits or diseases that are more prevalent in people of some races, they depend on the social definitions of race in order to pick out the members of the race they are studying.

The colloquial association of "blood" with race, as in the expressions, "She has black blood" or "He has some Indian blood" is no more than a metaphor, left over from the nineteenth-century pseudosciences of race. The four major human blood groups were identified in the early 1900s and it has been known since then that these blood types do not correspond to membership in races. There is some correspondence over the surface of the globe between geographical areas and blood types, but this is no more than a loose statistical association. We do think about the main racial groups as having originated in specific continental areas, such as Caucasians from northern Europe, Negroes from Africa, Asians from Asia, and Indians from the Americas. However, human populations have been in constant movement all over the globe for millions of years. And, the ordinary idea of race purports to tell us something about people as they are now, not about where their ancestors may have lived at some time in the past. Also, geographical origins of ancestors could not be reliable indicators of race because all races have been present on all continents over recorded history. Furthermore, most anthropologists now believe that human beings originated in Africa.

Racial membership has been culturally associated with some inherited physical characteristics, such as skin color and types of facial features, but these traits are no different in principle from other physical traits that have no racial significance, such as height. Moreover, the traits that are considered racial traits do not all get inherited together for any race, but are subject to dispersal and recombination each time a child is conceived.

Not only is there no general characteristic that determines racial membership, but the specific traits of skin color, hair texture, and bone structure vary more within any of the main racial groups than they do between any two racial groups. Indeed, scientists now speak of *populations* when referring to groups that the layperson would call races. Such populations may share more of some inherited physical traits than other populations. But the distribution of these traits within the membership of a population changes over generations and the human physical trait boundaries between populations cannot be sharply drawn. Even when the physical traits that are considered racial traits are compared within the general human population, they represent very small variations in genetic material, on the order of one ten-thousandth of all human genetic material.

What the foregoing amounts to is that there is no scientific basis for our idea of race as a human biological difference. Race, as something general about a person or a group, is a social overlay on actual physical traits. This is not to deny that people perceive what they think are racial traits or that race has a powerful social reality. But it means that what we think of as race is solely a matter of convention and imagination. We follow a convention of imagining the existence of races and sorting people into these imaginary categories. Once this realization of the imaginary nature of race sinks in, the human differences that are attributed to race have to be explained and understood in other terms. The physical differences of skin, hair, and bone that have been associated with race are not important enough, in relation to biological function, to require a deep explanation. However, many of the intellectual and moral differences that have been attributed to race are very important in terms of social status and individual well-being and it is those alleged differences that require careful study.

C. THE CULTURAL MEANINGS OF RACE

Even though race does not have the biological foundation it is assumed to have in common sense, not only is race very important in the United States but most adult Americans know what race they are and how to sort other people into their appropriate races. The question is, how do they—we—do that if there is greater physical variation within races than between races? Generally, people rely on the race of their close family members as a source of their own racial identity. And they generally rely on physical appearance for classifying others. That is, we have fairly clear images, in our minds and presented to us through the mass media, of how blacks, whites, Asians, and Indians are "supposed" to look. We expect people of our own and different races to conform to these images, and most of the time they seem to do so. Nonetheless, the images or stereotypes of racial appearance have varied historically and geographically in the United States and they do not work for classifying people who do not look "typical."

When physical appearance is ambiguous or atypical, the race of kin, of parents and other forebears, is the determining factor for racial classification. This family-inheritance aspect of race is also at work in determining the race of people whose appearance is racially "clear." It's just that if someone looks black and has black kin, or looks white and has white kin, there need be no explicit reference to the race of his or her ancestors. The ambiguous cases draw out the formal basis that underlines all racial classification. The formal basis for black and white racial identity amounts to this:

> *Black:* A person is black if he or she has a black ancestor anywhere in family history. This is known as the *"one-drop rule"* of black classification because it is based on a myth that one drop of "black blood" is sufficient to determine racial blackness. The one-drop rule is a legacy of nineteenth-century ideas of racial essences that results in *hypodescent* for racial mixture. A social system of hypodescent in cases of racial mixture means that offspring have the race of the parent with the lower racial status. Thus, Americans with both white and black ancestry are always officially classified as black and often encouraged to identify as black in personal and social contexts.

> *White:* A person is white if he or she has no black ancestry anywhere in family history. This means that in order to be white, a person has to be purely white. This is a condition impossible to prove because it would be *proving a negative,* in this case the absence of black ancestors. Before about 1900, definitions of whiteness were less restricted in some states because definitions of blackness rested on having one black grandparent, great-grandparent, or great-great-grandparent. This meant that someone could be white if he or she had a black ancestor one generation back from the generation in which a black ancestor would result in being black. (For example, in a state such as Virginia, where one black grandparent determined blackness, someone with one black great-grandparent and no known black ancestry more recent than that would have been classified as white.)

The formal one-drop rule definitions of black and white race that have been in effect during the twentieth century posit those two races as *logical contradictories* of one another. This entails that everyone is either black or white and that no one is both. However, it has been acknowledged since at least the beginning of the nineteenth century that other races besides black and white exist, so black and white cannot be logical contradictories. Therefore, the formal definitions are misleading, if not actually false.

Like the definitions of black and white, American cultural definitions of Asian and Indian rely on physical appearance and the race of ancestors. Indigenous American Indian cultures did not have biological concepts of race, and rules for tribal membership allowed generously for adoption into tribes other than those to which one or both biological parents belonged. However, because American Indians have entitlements based on treaty law, the U.S. federal government has sometimes imposed requirements for *blood quanta* of at least 50 percent ancestry from one tribe in order to be classified as an Indian. As a result of this policy, and due to loyalty to traditional cultural identities, many American Indian tribes have developed their own criteria for *full bloods.*

Asian Americans have been present in the United States since the mid-nineteenth century. Since that time, new immigrants have been sources of cheap labor and those born here have met with varied barriers to success. However, Asian Americans have not been as visible as American blacks or American Indians in *liberatory* literary and activist traditions that resist dominance by the white majority. At this time, Asian American groups include Cambodian, Chinese, Japanese, Filipino, Hmong and Laotian, Indian, Korean, Pacific Islander, Thai, and Vietnamese. Whether, and to what extent, these groups are perceived as one race depends on where they live and other specific cultural contexts.

Despite the formal one-drop rule definitions of American blackness and whiteness, in reality there is considerable racial mixture in this country. Only a minority of American Indians can prove they are full bloods; half of all Asian Americans marry non-Asians; approximately 6 percent of all whites have some black ancestry; approximately 90 percent of American blacks have nonblack ancestry; and the so-called Hispanic population has included wide racial variations of black, white, and Indian for hundreds of years. Still, few Americans choose to identify as mixed race and the idea of mixed race as a positive identity is relatively new. That Americans still use a system of three or four main races despite these commonly known facts about mixed race suggests either that the false nineteenth-century biological theory of racial essences is deeply embedded in "*folk* wisdom," or else that Americans suspend their rational disbeliefs about this theory for *pragmatic* reasons, or both.

Where the false nineteenth-century biological theory of racial essences is still believed, it is appropriate to refer to the scientific evidence against it, or rather, the lack of scientific evidence for it. This lack of evidence for biological race is not proof that such evidence will never be found. Nonetheless, and this is the conceptual point worth taking, most folk ideas about race are based on the false assumption that the evidence already exists.

Pragmatic reasons for believing in racial categories have always been fairly obvious from the standpoint of the group supporting the belief. Black slavery was accepted by the founders of the U.S. Constitution at a time when it was believed that all human beings had natural rights to freedom. It was written into the Constitution that for purposes of electing representatives based on population size, each black slave would be counted as two-thirds of a person. One way to justify slavery was to insist that blacks were inferior or incomplete human beings. Slavery, segregation, and other forms of injustice against blacks benefited whites economically, politically, and socially at the expense of blacks. Beliefs in human differences based on natural divisions of race were thus a convenient basis on which to *rationalize* unjust treatment that had motives of self-interest which could not otherwise be admitted or defended. The systematic theft of American Indian land and the destruction of native cultures, as well as the exploitation of the cheap labor of Asian immigrants, were similarly rationalized by myths of white racial superiority.

However, there is another side to this pragmatic coin of racial categorization. Nonwhite Americans who have been categorized in biological racial terms have found it useful to use their categories as *identities* from which to protest and resist injustice based on race. Nineteenth-century pseudoscience falsely connected unsubstantiated ideas of biological race with ideas of less advanced or degenerate inherited cultural traits and practices. Speculation was substituted for empirical methodology and connections were made between biology and culture that had no empirical or logical justification. There was no biological foundation even for ideas of biological race. But, the groups thus racialized have included positive and valued aspects of their cultures as part of their racial identities. Indeed, what black Americans often mean by the word *race* is a shared history of survival and struggle. American Indians, when they identify as *full-bloods,* often use the racial classification to indicate loyalty to traditional Indian religious beliefs and ways of living, although identities based on *indigenism* are independent of EuroAmerican classifications. Asian Americans also have group and individual interests in preserving traditional lifestyles and religions, although they have less often presented themselves as racially distinct on that basis.

The pragmatic importance of racial identification, for all groups, also derives from an association of racial identity with family relations. Almost all human beings claim to value their family members and their family relationships. The false biological concept of race was attached to real, physical, inherited traits. These physical inherited traits are anchored in family descent, which is also real.

The real and fulfilling, political, cultural, and familial associations with racial classification and belonging suggest that not all the connotations and associations of race are ungrounded or humanly diminishing. Therefore, care and skill must be used in dissolving the ignorant and unjust aspects of racial classification. The important question to consider and reconsider is this: Do differences among human groups require a *taxonomy* or classification scheme that creates the kind of strong divisions associated with the idea of race in the false biological sense?

D. DISCUSSION QUESTIONS

1. Given the scientific problems with race, are you convinced there is no such thing as race?

2. What difference, if any, does the lack of a scientific foundation for race make in how you think about race?

3. Suppose that next year, all redheaded people were defined as a separate race and there were laws against their intermarriage with those of different hair color. Could redheads become a race, in time?

4. Do the folk definitions of black and white make sense to you?

5. Given the varied history of race and the problems with race in the biological sciences, how would you explain what race is to an intelligent child?

E. RECOMMENDED READING

For an account of the meaning of the word *race* in the ancient world, see M. I. Finley, *Ancient Slavery and Modern Ideology.* A discussion of early modern philosophic ideas of race can be found in Naomi Zack, *Bachelors of Science: Seventeenth Century Identity, Then and Now,* chapter 12. Mark Twain's *The Tragedy of Pudd'nhead Wilson* depicts a clash between the idea of race as biological and the experience of race as cultural in nineteenth-century America. Stephen Jay Gould, in *The Mismeasure of Man,* documents the errors and fraud in nineteenth-century scientific studies of race. Nancy Leys Stepan compares the mismeasure of race to false ideas of female gender in "Race and Gender: The Role of Analogy in Science," in David Theo Goldberg, ed., *Anatomy of Racism.* See also, Stepan's *The Idea of Race in Science: Great Britain, 1800–1950.* Nineteenth-century myths of race are further discussed in William Stanton's *The Leopard's Spots: Scientific Attitudes Toward Race in America, 1819–59.* See Derrick Bell's *And We Are Not Saved: The Elusive Quest for Racial Justice,* chapter 1, for discussion of the "two-thirds person" status of black slaves in the U.S. Constitution as it was originally framed.

Analyses of the scientific emptiness of race are offered in: K. Anthony Appiah, *In My Father's House,* and "Race, Culture, Identity," in K. Anthony Appiah and Amy Gutman, *Color Consciousness: The Political Morality of Race;* Nancy Holmstrom, "Race, Gender and Human Nature," in Naomi Zack, ed., *RACE/SEX: Their Sameness, Difference and Interplay;* Richard C. Lewontin, Steven Rose and Leon J. Kamin, *Not In Our Genes;* and Naomi Zack, *Race and Mixed Race,* chapter 2, and "Race and Philosophic Meaning," in Naomi Zack, ed., *RACE/SEX.* There are classic articles on the separation of ideas of biological race from ideas of culture in *Race, Science and Society,* edited by Leo Kuper.

R. Fred Wacker documents the changing meaning of race in American social science in *Ethnicity, Pluralism and Race.* The history of the American one-drop rule is presented in Joel Williamson's *New People* and F. James Davis's *Who is Black?*

Terry P. Wilson documents American Indian racial criteria in "Blood Quantum: Native American Mixed Bloods," in Maria P. P. Root, ed., *Racially Mixed People in America.* The role of appearance for racial classification in theory is discussed by J. Angelo Corlett in "Parallels of Ethnicity and Gender," in Naomi Zack, ed., *RACE/SEX.* Mariella Squire-Hakey examines American Indian experience of the importance of appearance for American Indian classification in "Yankee Imperialism and Imperialist Nostalgia," in Naomi Zack, ed., *American Mixed Race: The Culture of Microdiversity*. Carlos Fernández compares North and South American concepts of race based on European Protestant versus Roman Catholic attitudes toward foreigners, in "La Raza and The Melting Pot," in Maria P. P. Root, ed., *Racially Mixed People in America*.

Positive constructions of racial identity occupy most of the liberatory literature on race. In particular, see: Leonard Harris, ed., *The Philosophy of Alain Locke* and John Langston Gwaltney's documentation of core black identities in *Drylongso: A Self-Portrait of Black America*. Primary sources of writings in black liberation are presented in Joanne Grant's *Black Protest: History, Documents and Analyses, 1619–Present*.

Literary reflections on Asian and American Indian experiences of difference are Maxine Hong Kingston's memoir of Chinese American identity in *Woman Warrior,* and the collected stories of Native American cultural identities in Craig Lesley, ed., *Talking Leaves: Contemporary Native American Short Stories*. On contemporary Native American liberation philosophies and activism, see: Ward Churchill, *Indians Are Us?* and Ward Churchill, ed., *From a Native Son: Selected Essays on Indigenism, 1985–1995;* Ernest L. Schusky, *The Right to be Indian*. The possibility of united Asian American identity is explored by Yen Le Espiritu in *Asian American Panethnicity: Bridging Institutions and Identities*. The relatively recent focus on political empowerment among Asian Americans is presented in a microcosm by the Illinois Advisory Committee to the United States Commission on Civil Rights in *Civil Rights Issues Facing Asian Americans in Metropolitan Chicago*.

Y OU KNOW THE STEREOTYPES AND INSULTING NAMES
ASSOCIATED WITH MEMBERS OF THE RACE TO WHICH YOU
BELONG. WHEN SOMEONE OF YOUR SAME RACE JOKINGLY APPLIES
THEM TO YOU, YOU MAY NOT LIKE IT BUT YOU DON'T GET ANGRY. THE
EFFECT IS DIFFERENT IF THE SOURCE IS SOMEONE OF A DIFFERENT
RACE. WHY IS THAT?

CHAPTER 2

THE SOCIAL REALITY
OF RACE

INTRODUCTION

We've seen in Chapter 1 that the notion of human races as distinct biological breeds
has no foundation in physical science. In contemporary society, especially in educated or "enlightened" subcultures, there is broad agreement that the findings of the
physical sciences are the most reliable source of information about physical reality.
To say that race in the physical sense has no foundation in science is to say that race
in the physical sense is not real. Since by race, most Americans mean something
physical, the lack of a foundation in science means that race is not real. Period.

However, if you told most people that race is not real, the typical reaction
would probably be a blank stare. Most Americans believe that race is real and there
is a great deal invested in that belief throughout American culture, now, and going
back several hundred years. This false belief in the reality of race as physical difference, together with all the things that have been done based on that belief, gives race
in the physical sense a *social reality.* If the social reality of race were not as powerful as it is, the simple realization of its lack of physical reality would justify refusing
to think or talk about race at all. At the very least, we might begin putting the general
word "race" and its specific types, such as "black," "white," and "Asian," in quotation
marks. However, those gestures would have no impact on the social reality of race
unless everyone performed them, and that is unlikely to happen soon. So, in order to
think about race, we have to think about the social reality of race. At the same time,
we need to keep in the back of our minds the truth that the keystone of that reality,
namely the belief that race is real in the physical sense, is false.

While Americans believe that biological races exist, many also insist that racial
differences are not important. What they mean by this is that racial difference *ought*
not to make a difference in how people are rewarded and punished for what they do,
or in how people are valued as human beings. Section A offers some clarification of

the differences between morally *egalitarian* positions on racial difference. These *normative* positions describe how things should be, rather than how they are. Some *descriptive* positions on the social reality of race are examined in Section B. These positions differ depending on who is doing the describing. Therefore, it might be that the only way to reconcile these positions is to eliminate the idea of race. However, tigers once ridden must be dismounted with care, and Section C addresses the practical problems with an *eliminative* position on race.

A. NORMATIVE POSITIONS ON THE SOCIAL REALITY OF RACE

Let's say that anyone who believes in the biological reality of races is a *racialist.* A racialist might think that the differences between races are important or unimportant as human traits. A racialist who thinks that racial differences are unimportant is unlikely to be a *racist. Racism* is the subject of Chapter 5, but we should note here that it involves ill will and/or harmful action toward people on the basis of their race. A racialist who thinks that human differences due to race are important might or might not be a racist.

Some racialists are *racial determinists.* They believe that as a result of belonging to a biological race, individuals are determined to have certain nonracial traits. These traits generally correspond to the aptitudes and skills, virtues and vices that nineteenth-century hierarchical theories associated with the different races, ranking the white race highest. However, most Americans, due to wide-ranging personal experience or their awareness of scientific findings, now accept that human talents and morality are evenly distributed across and within all races. That is, most racialists now acknowledge that the inheritance of biological race is not accompanied by the inheritance of predetermined sets of aptitudes and skills or virtues and vices. Therefore, the theory of racial determinism is either false or else it is the normative position that people of different races *ought to have* different nonracial traits. It is difficult to see how the normative position of racial determinism could be defended, because it looks like what most people would at present call a racist position.

Let's assume that the racialist we are considering is not a racist. Many nonracist American racialists are *egalitarians.* They believe that racial differences in themselves do not have an effect on fundamental human worth and, that therefore, racial differences ought not to affect how people are treated by others, how they regard themselves, or how well they do in society. But even a position of racial equality based on universal human equality, or *universalism,* is not a description of how things are but of how they ought to be. This is because in the real world, it is often very difficult to preserve universal human equality in the face of perceived racial differences. The egalitarian might insist that, despite what happens to people on the basis of racial difference, they are nevertheless equal as people. Such insistence might be based on an abstract, universal idea of a generic human being that lies at the core of everyone, regardless of race. The idea of this kind of equality would have an appeal to many, especially those who were religious. But inequalities based on racial difference do not affect core human equality, so it is difficult to see how a belief in such equality could be used as an argument for social change. Furthermore, those who unjustly treat people differently based on race may be prepared to ignore core human equality, so it is not likely to motivate them to behave justly. Therefore, the assertion of universal core human equality is somewhat irrelevant to practical inequalities based on race.

But suppose that a racialist egalitarian has a more concrete idea of what a human being is, so that the universal human being is not a core human being without racial traits, but a concrete human being who is always a member of some distinct race. In that case, the egalitarian would have to assert that the nonracial differences associated with particular races, such as social or economic status, ought not to exist. The egalitarian would then be committed to changes in the social reality of race that would result in equality. Before we can consider what kind of changes might be necessary to bring about equality in society where there is now inequality based on racial difference, we need to be able to describe the social reality of race.

B. Descriptive Positions on the Social Reality of Race

The social reality of race is made up of the ways in which human life differs within the same culture, at the same historical time, according to racial classification. The way that members of racial groups perceive their own and other races is also part of the social reality of race. This reality is more than a matter of difference in the sense of variety, because some racial groups are dominant over others. Dominant groups have more of the goods of society such as money, material possessions, security (including personal safety), education, fulfilling employment, leisure time, and social status. As a result, members of dominant racial groups have more power in society, and the recognition of this power results in their greater *authority.* In the United States the dominant racial group has always been white, and whites generally have more authority than nonwhites.

The ways in which the social reality of race are described depends on the racial perspective of the person doing the describing. General descriptions from the perspectives of whites, blacks, Indians, and Asians seem to unfold along the following lines.

Although most American whites are racialists, race is not the most important social factor in their daily experience. Race is not a problem for most whites in terms of a history of being dominated, or as a present barrier to the development of their aptitudes and the attainment of social goods. From a white perspective, the social reality of race could be described as an element in human interaction that involves the problems faced by nonwhite minorities and the problems faced by whites in dealing with nonwhite minorities. Since whites are currently the majority as well as the dominant group, and much of American life is still segregated by race, many whites are not personally affected by race. They can grow up, get an education, work, choose companions and spouses, raise families, buy houses, get medical care, go on vacation, retire, and die, without having anything important to contend with on the grounds of race. Among themselves, whites need not be aware of themselves in racial terms at all. So long as all the important people in their lives are white, they have no need to think of themselves in terms of race. In this sense for whites, among whites, race might as well not exist.

While most American whites acknowledge that nonwhites have been badly treated in the past, they assume that American society is presently egalitarian and that justice exists for nonwhites. Most whites acknowledge that nonwhites were treated unjustly in the past, particularly blacks subjected to slavery and segregation. But this injustice is widely assumed to have been corrected by a steady progression of laws, constitutional amendments, and court decisions upholding the civil rights of nonwhites. More than a few whites now believe that the greatest present racial injustice in the United States is *affirmative action* policy that favors nonwhites over whites.

In general, American white society in the late twentieth century has honored and idealized American Indians. Also, in general, Asian Americans are perceived by whites to be a successful racial minority because they have been willing to work hard and they value education. But these are recent historical developments. American colonists viewed Indians as ignorant heathens, and the nineteenth-century economic and military expansion westward was accompanied by images of Indians as warlike and uncivilized. Asians were shunned by white society in all respects, except as a source of cheap labor, until the second half of the twentieth century.

Complaints of racism from nonwhites are often considered unjustified by whites. Welfare assistance to inner-city blacks and court enforcement of Indian sovereignty on reservations may be viewed as undeserved privileges financed by hardworking taxpayers who happen to be mostly white. Asian American socioeconomic success may be resented and viewed as the result of unfair cultural advantages or group solidarity in an individualistic society.

It is odd and surprising for whites to be insulted, hated, obstructed, or excluded on the grounds of their race. If it does happen, it may make them aware of being racially distinctive or different, for the first time. Many whites are not aware that they belong to the dominant racial group, and they have no conscious intention of harming anyone based on racial difference. Accordingly, they are likely to be shocked and infuriated by antiwhite injury that is based on race. As noted earlier, affirmative action has been criticized because it favors nonwhites over whites.

The description of the social reality of race is very different from a black perspective. Blacks have a tradition of awareness of the ways in which being black influences how they grow up, the education accessible to them, where they work, the stability of their family life, the kind of housing and medical care obtainable, and their social status and authority. They know that as a group, they not only do not belong to the dominant majority but also share a history of slavery, segregation, and discrimination implemented by whites on the basis of racial difference.

Black history is embedded in U.S. history, throughout which the federal government upheld local oppression of blacks. In Chapter 1, we mentioned the "two-thirds person" status of black slaves under the U.S. Constitution. In the *Dred Scott* case in 1857, the U.S. Supreme Court ruled that Negroes were not U.S. citizens. It was a crime in slave-owning states to teach slaves how to read or write, and it wasn't until the 1954 *Brown v. Board of Education* case that blacks were legally entitled to equal, integrated educational opportunities. Before then, in *Plessy v. Ferguson* (1896) the Supreme Court had upheld segregation based on community custom. On the basis of historical examples such as these, as well as ongoing inequities in the administration of justice, ***critical race theorists*** who study American culture from a black racial perspective believe that antiblack racism in the United States is an integral part of a capitalistic economic system and a false egalitarian political system that favors whites.

At present, blacks value many of the same social goods that come more easily to whites and they believe that they do not have the same opportunities as whites to acquire them. Many blacks believe that one reason for this barrier is that whites have not implemented all the legal changes that were intended to ensure equal opportunity after the Civil Rights movement(s). A second reason is that blacks, in developing skills for succeeding in society, also have to contend with the results of centuries of poverty and oppression. From a black perspective, the general effect is that racial difference is a constant, important aspect of daily life that continues to work against blacks, in every aspect of their lives.

As with African Americans, the history of Native Americans is an integral part of American history. However, the situation of Native Americans is probably more complex than that of other nonwhite minorities because, in principle, Indian nations are "dependent sovereignties" within the United States. Since the nineteenth century, these nations have been defined, redefined, legislated out of existence, or encouraged to pursue self-rule. Treaty law was largely manipulated at the will of Euro-American interests in Indian lands and the resources on and under those lands. Efforts at imposed assimilation have not been successful: although over 60 percent of Native Americans now live off reservations, with many in urban areas, rates of unemployment are often over 50 percent.

Contemporary Indian activists affirm traditional values according to their specific Indian nationalities. They view their people as victims of ***genocide,*** both physical and cultural, and express strong repudiation of EuroAmerican socioeconomic progress, especially insofar as that progress accelerates the destruction of natural environments. The cultural differences between nontechnological traditional Indian societies and modern American capitalist society probably run deeper than can be described in terms of perspectives deriving from racial categories.

Although white society has ***valorized*** Indians, the Indians in question have not been actual living Indians who struggle in poverty on reservations or in urban ghettos. Rather, the honor has usually gone to past Indians who fought bravely and were massacred or driven off their land, or to Indian characters in novels and movies. Therefore, contemporary Indian writers are likely to view such white valorization as cultural ***appropriation.*** In substituting EuroAmerican fantasies of Indians for historical Indians, the reality of Indian life can be ignored by whites. For many Indian thinkers, this denial of Indian culture is no different in principle from nineteenth-century direct genocidal policy against Indians. For nearly a century, in addition to the massacre of Indian people, Indian culture was directly attacked through laws that prohibited the practice of indigenous languages, religions, and livelihoods.

Unlike blacks, whose ancestors were brought to the United States in chains, and American Indians, whose ancestors were here before all other groups, Asian Americans have ancestors who largely chose to come to the United States. Some came for economic opportunity, others to avoid political oppression. During the nineteenth century, Chinese immigrants to the U.S. were part of a worldwide population referred to as *overseas Chinese,* consisting of poor single men. Extreme legal restrictions were placed on Asian immigration during the late nineteenth and early twentieth centuries, and for decades Chinese women were not admitted to the United States. Chinese immigrants were known for hard work, business acumen, and great thrift, but they were denied U.S. citizenship as well as professional employment. This situation began to improve after the 1920s and Chinese Americans are now considered more successful in the professions than any other ethnic group, based on their numerical proportion of the population.

But unlike Europeans, all of whom eventually assimilated into the dominant white majority, Asian Americans have generally not completely assimilated. Part of the reason is their desire to perpetuate traditional cultures. Contemporary activists in Asian communities have focused on the ways in which Asians need to organize to achieve political representation commensurate with full civil liberty. Some writers claim that until recently, many Asian American communities have been attuned to political issues in their countries of origin rather than to American civic and political events that have direct influence on their lives in the United States.

The main external barrier to full Asian assimilation has been racial classification as nonwhite. In addition, many Asians assert that no matter how many generations their families have been Americans, the white majority perceives them as foreigners. The federal government interned Japanese Americans in California during World War II, ostensibly because the United States was at war with Japan. But many Asian Americans and others view this as a deeply alienating episode that expressed American xenophobia and anti-Asian racism.

Asian Americans whose families have been in the United States for generations or whose families recently immigrated with wealth and education have succeeded economically and attained respected professional and social status. Nonetheless, some claim that this success has invisible ceilings beyond tangible rewards for technical expertise. Asians who presently arrive without money and education still have to work and study long hours to get out of poverty. Positions against Asian immigration have reemerged in recent years, either because the poor work too hard for other groups to compete against them successfully, or because financially successful Asian Americans have become increasingly visible as owners of property and businesses. Thus, the acceptance of Asian Americans in American economic life has been sufficiently grudging and resentful to justify feelings that they are not welcomed and valued by the majority of white Americans.

It might be argued that the different situations of whites, blacks, Indians, and Asians can be traced to something as simple as skin color. According to an explanation in terms of *colorism,* white is the most preferred color and black the least preferred color, with the skin colors of Indians and Asians falling between. On this view, the basis of the social reality of race is differences in physical appearance that

Americans perceive so habitually they aren't even aware of doing so. It doesn't matter that skin color is a bad predictor of other human traits, of social background, or even of race as it is officially defined, because few people are able to think beyond skin color. This skin-color hypothesis could account for why whites have remained dominant, Indians have been distantly valorized by whites, Asians have been successful in white culture, and blacks have remained at the bottom.

However, the problem with the colorist explanation of the social reality of race is what it ignores: the wide range of skin color within black, Asian, and Native American classifications; the near-genocide of American Indians; the fact that some blacks have lighter skin than some Asians and Indians as well as some whites.

The different racial perspectives on the social reality of race in the United States all have to be taken into account if one is committed to a concrete egalitarianism. If belonging to one or another racial group results in a distinctive view of racial difference, then who is to say which group's view is the right one? One would have to allow that each group's view is the right view for that group. This kind of tolerance of difference in social perspective can lead to a view of society as a whole as *pluralistic.* On the other hand, a universal egalitarian might insist that since these different perspectives sometimes contradict each other, they cannot all be accurate—at least not at the same time. Because there are no fair grounds for choosing any one over the others, all the perspectives ought to be discarded in favor of one that could be shared by everyone. The only way to do this is to *eliminate* the false concept of biological race. Without that concept, no one would be able to see the members of groups different from their own, as different enough to discriminate against, react to discrimination from, or resent. That is, perhaps we can simply eliminate the false concept of biological race and start from scratch on an unbiased and equal basis.

C. Problems with Eliminativism

Cases for racial eliminativism can be made based on principle or on consequences. On principle, the concept of biological race is false and that in itself is reason to eliminate it. Eliminating race would be a simple matter of spreading the truth about the nonexistence of race, beginning with what children are taught in elementary school.

The problem with this "argument from truth" is that it's one thing to proclaim that something is true and quite another to insist that people accept that truth. The First Amendment to the U.S. Constitution guarantees freedom of thought, belief, and opinion as part of free speech. Therefore, the truth about race cannot be imposed on Americans against their will. Since belief in races is part of *received opinion,* parents and even teachers would strongly resist an educational program to eliminate ideas of race. Insofar as members of different racial groups believe in the existence of their races, many would strongly resist any forced elimination of racial thinking, especially if they benefit from recognition as being members of the race they are—which almost everyone does, in one way or another. That is, enforcement of the truth about race would violate the protected right of free speech, which means that it could not be done in this country. Religious freedom offers an apt comparison here. It is impossible to prove the existence of God based on scientific evidence, but no one therefore proposes that people ought not to be allowed to worship and practice their religions.

A *consequentialist* argument for eliminating race can be derived from a concrete egalitarian position that people ought to be equal in society. Since human beings are equal in aptitude, it is the perception of racial difference that results in social inequalities based on race. History has proved that it is impossible for Americans to think in terms of racial difference without being influenced by the false nineteenth-century hierarchical theories of race. If Americans were unable to think in these racial terms or to speak the language of race, then they would be unable to behave unfairly on the basis of racial difference. Ideas of race ought to be eliminated because the consequences would be good.

There are several problems with this line of reasoning. First, there is no reason why people cannot have false (i.e., scientifically ungrounded) ideas of racial difference that do not carry all the baggage of nineteenth-century hierarchical theories. Some Americans do have such benign ideas of race. Second, if race is unreal, that is, a cultural fiction, then people must be using other things to pick out the different racial groups for unequal treatment, other things such as economic status, culture, country of ancestral origin, and so forth. Without a concept of race, these other things will still be there. This suggests that the problem is not so much with the false folk idea of race as with the uses people make of that idea due to greed and cruelty. But greed and cruelty will not automatically be eliminated if the idea of race is eliminated. For example, even if Native Americans were not racialized at present, Euro-American economic interests in their lands would not change, and neither would indigenist attempts to resist those interests.

The eliminativist might regroup in the face of these objections and formulate other arguments from principle or consequences. For instance, it could be said that Americans have overused their unique cultural structures of racial difference to generate public debates, with the result that more important issues such as poverty, destruction of natural environments, and treatment of drug addiction have been neglected. Giving race a rest might free up energy for dealing with these problems. If the problems masked by race would remain when racial categories were no longer in use, then getting rid of these categories would make it possible to confront those problems more directly and openly. Some writers have suggested that the fundamental problem of human relations, generally, is an "us-versus-them" mentality that has an outlet in false notions of racial difference. So why not get rid of the imaginary differences and deal with that problem whenever it comes up?

Thus far, we have been discussing proactive eliminative positions. Since the concept of race as we know it did not always exist historically, it could pass out of history on its own without strenuous intellectual effort. People could stop believing in race due to changes in life circumstances. One such change might be an expansion of the number of racial categories, or an increase in the number of individuals who were unable or unwilling to classify themselves, or to be classified by others, in terms of the three or four currently accepted races. Recent increases in the number of mixed-race people in America, as well as spontaneous grassroots movements in favor of mixed-race classifications, suggest this type of change. Mixed race is the subject of Chapter 3.

D. DISCUSSION QUESTIONS

1. What do you think is the most important aspect of the social reality of race in the United States at this time?

2. Why do people of the same race sit together in college classrooms?

3. Is there any form of racial determinism that can be defended, in your view?

4. How would your life or the lives of people you know change if race were eliminated?

5. What are some moral rules that you think everyone ought to follow in relating to people of different races?

E. RECOMMENDED READING

For criticism of racial determinism in the social reality of race, see Ashley Montagu's *Man's Most Dangerous Myth: The Fallacy of Race;* and *The Concept of Race.* On the formation of specifically American racial social reality, see Yehudi O. Webster, *The Racialization of America.* For broad and cross-cultural information on the social reality of race, see Oliver C. Cox, *Caste, Class and Race.* On the social reality of race in Latin America, see Richard Graham, ed., *The Idea of Race in Latin America, 1870–1940.* On the formation of racial groups as social entities, see L. Singer, "Ethnogenesis and Negro-Americans Today," in *Social Research.* For philosophical analysis of Western political theory in relation to slavery, see Tommy L. Lott, ed., *Subjugation and Bondage: Critical Essays on Slavery and Social Philosophy.*

Classic sources on the social reality of black race are: W. E. B. Du Bois, *The Souls of Black Folk* and Franz Fanon, *Black Skin, White Masks.* See also Lewis R. Gordon's contemporary interpretation of Fanon in *Fanon and the Crisis of European Man: An Essay on Philosophy and the Human Sciences.* Sources for the legal history of black-white relations in the U.S. are Derrick Bell's *And We Are Not Saved: The Elusive Quest for Racial Justice* and Joanne Grant's *Black Protest: History, Documents and Analyses 1619–Present.* Useful recent works on legal studies and black critical race theory include: Patricia J. Williams, *The Rooster's Egg: On the Persistence of Prejudice;* Richard Delgado, *Critical Race Theory: The Cutting Edge;* Mari Matsuda, Charles R. Lawrence and Kimberle Williams, *Words that Wound: Critical Race Theory, Assaultive Speech, and the First Amendment.*

Further critical contemporary sources on black social reality include Paul Gilroy, *The Black Atlantic: Modernity and Double Consciousness* and Patricia Williams, *The Alchemy of Race and Rights.* Lewis R. Gordon examines the problematic aspects of existence for black people in white society in *Bad Faith and Antiblack Racism* and (ed.) *Existence in Black: An Anthology of Existentialist Black Philosophy.*

On Asian American social reality, see: Robert Olen Butler's *A Good Scent from a Strange Mountain: Stories* (Vietnamese); Ronald Takaki, *Strangers from a Different Shore: A History of Asian Americans;* Maria Hong, *Growing up Asian American: An Anthology.*

Contemporary activist sources on Native American social racial reality are: Baird J. Callicott, *In Defense of the Land Ethic;* Ward Churchill, *Struggle for the Land;* Susan Clements, "Five Arrows" in Naomi Zack, ed., *American Mixed Race: The Culture of Microdiversity;* Peter Nabokov, ed., *Native American Testimony: A Chronicle of Indian-White Relations from Prophecy to the Present;* Russell Thornton, *American Indian Holocaust Survival: A Population History Since 1492.* On U.S. government public policy toward Native Americans, see: Fremont J. Lyden and Lyman H. Legters, eds., *Native Americans and Public Policy.* On problems of Indian assimilation in urban areas, a recent source is Gregory W. Frazier's *Urban Indians: Drums from the Cities.* On indigenous philosophies and world views, see: Dennis Tedlock and Barbara Tedlock, eds., *Teachings from the American Earth;* D. M. Dooling and Paul Jordan-Smith, eds., *I Become Part of It: Sacred Dimensions in Native American Life.*

THE PERSON SITTING NEXT TO YOU ON AN AIRPLANE IS READING A NOVEL YOU JUST FINISHED. YOU BEGIN A CONVERSATION. THIS PERSON LOOKS BOTH BLACK AND WHITE OR MAYBE SOMETHING ELSE YOU CAN'T IDENTIFY. YOU ARE CURIOUS ABOUT WHAT RACE YOUR COMPANION IS BUT YOU THINK IT MIGHT BE RUDE TO ASK. WHY ARE YOU CURIOUS AND WHY MIGHT THE QUESTION BE RUDE?

CHAPTER 3

MIXED RACE

INTRODUCTION

If races were real, most people would be mixed, because there have been no lasting situations in history during which entire distinctive groups of people were isolated and bred exclusively within themselves. But races are not real, so racial mixture is not real either. However, most Americans think that races are real. And, they do not recognize the existence of mixed-race groups as categories distinct from the four major racial groups—for various reasons.

Traditionally, everyone with mixed black and white ancestry has been classified as black, regardless of their amount of white ancestry. From a black perspective, mixed black and whites have been routinely accepted as black, especially by black kin. While American blacks generally acknowledge racial mixture, they take mixed race to be a fact about blackness for some people, rather than an independent racial category. Historically, the white majority has been ambivalent about mixed-race classification. In some states during the nineteenth century, mixed black and white Americans with one-eighth or less degree of known black ancestry were legally white, and the U.S. census included mixed black-and-white categories such as *mulatto, quadroon,* and *octoroon.* About 1900, the one-drop rule became the law of the land for black classification, and by 1920, mixed black-and-white racial categories were deleted from the U.S. census. At the same time, the term *mulatto,* which originally meant "half black and half white," became a general label for anyone with any degree of black racial mixture. It has been estimated by anthropologists that 70 to 90 percent of American blacks have white ancestry and about 30 percent have Indian ancestry as well. When the census stopped classifying mixed black-and-white Americans as distinct categories within black, those ethnic groups that were previously considered distinct nonwhite, such as Italians, Poles, Spaniards, and Jews, were reclassified as white. Although almost all white Americans now accept these ethnic groups as white, many black Americans reserve the racial classification of white for northern European ethnic whites, such as Scandinavians, Germans, and British.

The situation of mixed race has a different structure for other nonwhite mixtures. Mixed Indians-and-whites have been rejected as Indian by the federal government in order to minimize Indian treaty *entitlements.* For example, when Indian tribes have accepted mixed-race Indians as Indians, the Bureau of Indian Affairs has often not recognized them as Indians because their *blood quantum* has been less than the required 50 percent heritage from one tribe. Since recognized tribal membership as full-blood has connoted full cultural status as Indian, some full-blooded Indians in western tribes carry laminated miniaturized photocopies of the documentation of this status as prized "I.D."

Eurasians have been more easily accepted as white by whites than as Asian by their kin of unmixed Asian ancestry. Indian-and-black and Asian-and-black Americans have been categorized as black by whites and met with varied degrees of acceptance and rejection by blacks, Asians, and Indians. Although American Indians did not have ideas of race before European colonization, and Asian Americans have different concepts of culture as race in their nations of origin, both groups have for the most part accepted the mainstream American system of racial classification.

It should be noted that historically, the state of Hawaii is an exception to the American system of monoracial classification. Hawaiians have a long cultural tradition of public recognition of a multiplicity of mixed-race groups, as well as more social acceptance of mixed-race individuals by all groups on the islands.

Mixed-race Americans are instances of *microdiversity,* because their racial difference exists on the level of an individual person, unlike the *diversity* that is acknowledged to exist between or among the four major racial groups. This microdiversity itself takes different forms. There is a difference between mixed-race people who know they are mixed because their grandparents or great-grandparents were not all members of the same race, and mixed-race people who know they are mixed because their parents are members of different races. First-generation mixed-race individuals are more likely to have intense personal experience of the problems of being mixed in a *monoracial* system and to demand recognition and respect on that basis. In 1967, the U.S. Supreme Court struck down all state laws prohibiting marriage between people of different races. At present, mixed-race births within marriage are the fastest growing segment of births broken down by race. Present generations of mixed-race Americans, as well as many of their parents, have been visible in grassroots organizations such as Project RACE (Reclassify All Children Equally) that advocates use of a mixed-race classification for schoolchildren on state levels. In most states, children who want to be classified as multiracial now have the option only of identifying as *"other."*

Scholars, psychologists, and other advocates such as members of AMEA (Association of MultiEthnic Americans) have testified before the U.S. Congress in favor of categories for mixed race on the U.S. census. There was a march in favor of federal recognition of mixed race, in Washington, D.C., in July 1995. Although these efforts have received broad media attention, and new academic work on mixed race has appeared in the 1980s and 1990s, thus far there is still no comprehensive official recognition of mixed race in the United States. We do not know exactly what the future will hold for mixed-race identity. Mixed-race Americans are an increasingly visible and vocal group. They remain minorities within minorities but their demands may be more fundamental to human rights and values than is reflected by their numbers alone. The purpose of this chapter is to consider some of the issues, for both individuals and society, that are involved in microdiversity.

Section A presents theoretical arguments in favor of mixed-race identity. Section B outlines different options for mixed-race identity. Section C is a consideration of the problems with mixed-race identity.

A. ARGUMENTS FOR MIXED-RACE IDENTITY

If people who think they are monoracial have a right to racial identities, then so ought people who are *biracial* or *multiracial* have that right. To deny mixed-race adults or children identities as mixed is to discriminate against them on racial grounds. Such discrimination is morally wrong, and on that basis, it should be illegal. However, so long as the existence of mixed race is not recognized by law, legally speaking, there is no discrimination.

Assuming that mixed race continues to be unrecognized within the United States, arguments for legal change could be based on international human rights. According to the *Universal Declaration of Human Rights* adopted by the General Assembly of the United Nations in 1948, all individuals have a right to choose their religions and beliefs, and no individual can be compelled to belong to an association. When it was assumed that racial identity was a simple matter of a natural category evident at birth, the idea of choice of racial identity would not have made sense. But now that we know race is at best a system of categories created by culture, there is no reason not to revise that system where it is inadequate or repressive for some individuals. Because race is not a natural biological category but something that people affirm or have imposed on them, it resembles a *creed.* Therefore, if people want to identify as racially mixed, they should be allowed to do so and respected for their choice, as part of their more general human rights to free speech and freedoms of creed and association.

Beside the international human rights arguments, issues of social and psychological *utility,* which includes harm and benefit as well as usefulness, are also relevant. If all mixtures between whites and nonwhites result in offspring being categorized as nonwhite, when nonwhites have lower status than whites, this reinforces the idea that nonwhite ancestry, especially black ancestry, is a special kind of defect. Black ancestry is the only kind of hereditary categorization that applies to an entire person solely because it applies to one ancestor. Furthermore, so long as mixed black-and-white racial identification is denied, racial mixtures between nonwhites, such as Indian and black, Indian and Asian, or Asian and black, are not taken seriously. Ignoring the different racial identities of children of nonwhite interracial unions has a depersonalizing and dehumanizing effect on them because it suggests that the unique aspects of their heritage and racial experience are nonexistent or unimportant.

Psychologically, knowing that one is of mixed race in a society that doesn't recognize and respect such a racial identity can seriously impair one's self-esteem and social functioning. Children growing up within mixed families may feel ashamed of their "irregular" racial makeup and may experience rejection and alienation in the wider social community.

The idea of monoracial identity has been attached to family inheritance and family descent for cultural reasons, not biological ones. But the result is an assumption that "real" families are monoracial. When children in biracial and multiracial families are not permitted to claim their full family inheritance, the emotionally stabilizing and interpersonally connective aspects of their family life are damaged. Because the culture does not recognize mixed race, monoracial family members may emotionally reject mixed-race children and exclude them from the broader family life. Thus, as things now stand, racially mixed children are denied a secure social identity and may also be denied those emotionally nourishing benefits of belonging to a family that monoracial children can take for granted.

Adolescents and adults who are racially mixed are put in the position of having to explain basic facts about themselves that those whose racial identities are recognized do not have to explain. The mixed-race person is often considered a strange and exotic object, not because most Americans are in fact unaware of the existence of mixed race, but because they know that there is no official public place for it. Mixed race is presently unacknowledged.

Finally, if mixed-race identities were recognized, the differences between the major racial groups would not be so distancing in human terms and it would be more difficult for people to think falsely about races as biologically distinct species or subspecies. This might eventually break down essentialist, all-or-none ideas about race. Since what people think of as race is in fact a fluid multiplicity of human typing that can change in one generation, a recognition of mixed race would generally result in a more flexible idea of what it is to be a human being. Such a change in how we think about people would make it possible for all individuals to be more expressive about their backgrounds and experience. The present requirement of fitting into rigid, stereotyped categories of appearance, belonging, and what one is expected to say about who one is racially, places an unnecessary stress on all human interactions. Mixed-raced people would be happier if their racial identities were recognized. Monoracial people would also benefit from the removal of some of the burdens that go along with maintaining rigid racial identities, such as obligations to conform and hostility toward races different from their own.

B. MIXED-RACE IDENTITY OPTIONS

Let's imagine that mixed race were generally recognized in the United States. It's not clear exactly how mixed-race people would or should identify themselves. Suppose that Jane's mother is white and her father is black and Indian. Jane could identify herself in rough fractional terms as one-third white, one-third black, and one-third Indian. Or she might choose to apply fractions more literally and identify herself as one-half white, one-quarter black, and one-quarter Indian.

On the other hand, Jane may not like presenting herself as "divided" in this way. She could insist that, as a result of a warm and close family life, she has experienced all the racial identities that belong to her parents. She may be unable to determine which "part" of herself is the half, third, or quarter that is white, black, or Indian. As a result, Jane's mixed-race identity could be *inclusive,* so that she identifies as white *and* black *and* Indian.

By contrast, suppose Jane's friend Dick, who is also black, white, and Indian, grew up on an Indian reservation and studied the oral traditions, ceremonies, and medical practices of his Indian grandparents. Dick wants to identify as a Lakota Sioux, a member of the tribe in which he is enrolled. However, Dick's half-brother Martin was not raised with his Indian relatives and he now lives in a city with their black father, stepmother, and step-siblings, who all identify as African American. Martin has declined tribal enrollment several times and identifies himself as black.

Now, let's return to the complexities of Jane's family life. Jane's parents divorce just after her sister Andrea is born, when Jane is sixteen and secure in her inclusive identity. Andrea grows up in a household headed by her white mother, so she does not have the same experience of black and Indian ancestry from their father that Jane did. When Andrea is eight her mother remarries, and her second husband is white. Suppose Andrea then wants to identify as white. In a society that overcame its one-drop rule by recognizing mixed race, should she be prohibited from this identification?

Meanwhile, Jane has completed her graduate work in French art history at the Sorbonne and she marries a fellow student, Johann, who is Dutch. They decide to live in Vermont, where Johann has been hired by a museum that has an excellent collection of eighteenth-century European landscape painters. Jane has been unable to satisfactorily explain the American racial system to her husband and decides to drop her own racial identity completely so they can raise their children as citizens of the world. When Andrea comes to visit them, she tells her sister and brother-in-law about BOMBS, an organization in which she is active in college (Brown's Organization of Multiracial and Biracial Students). Apparently, some members of BOMBS insist that they be identified generically as *mixed* without specifying exactly how they are mixed. Jane and Johann think this is similar to their idea of world citizenship in the human race, but Andrea insists it is distinctly American to be "mixed" in this way.

What these examples, and much of the literary and scholarly work on contemporary mixed race, suggest is that recognized mixed-race identity might take any or all of the following forms: *fractional, inclusive, traditional nonwhite, white, generic,* and *aracial.* Also, mixed-race individuals may want to change their racial identities as their life experience changes.

C. PROBLEMS WITH MIXED-RACE IDENTITY

The main problem with recognizing mixed-race identity in the United States is that it isn't the way we do things. Although customary and traditional practices are by no means automatically right—slavery was *customary* and *traditional* for hundreds of years—some things in human life seem to be universally decided by custom and tradition (which is custom over time). Globally, the ways in which human beings identify and are identified by race have been and still are decided by custom and tradition. Many different racial policies exist from country to country: In South America, racial mixture is an approved and accepted fact of life because it has been for hundreds of years. The Latin American expression *la raza*, "the race," makes of Latinos and Latinas one race, despite all their acknowledged mixtures of European, Indian, and African ancestry. In Brazil, although white racial appearance is preferred, racial identity and status can change upward toward white as mulattoes who otherwise do not appear white rise socioeconomically; this has been called the "lightening effect of money." In South Africa, the category *colored* is used to designate mixed race, and it is also a fact of daily life, duly announced in local newspapers, that people can petition the courts to have their race officially changed if their circumstances and the people they associate with change racially. In England, East Indians and Pakistani are known as black; in the United States, they are considered white or Asian. In China, the moral virtues associated with ethnic differences in cultural practices are presumed to be inherited. In India, social status based on membership in a rigid hierarchical caste system is inherited, much as black or white race is in the United States. These differences in what counts as race show that systems of racial classification are culturally relative, the result of long-established practices based on historical circumstances. Therefore, as a tradition that develops over time within a culture, a system of racial classification should be accepted as a fact of history. While such facts can be criticized, it is extremely difficult for individuals, small groups, or even governments to change them.

American racial identity according to the four major races is a type of identity that is anchored vertically in time. People have "roots" going back for generations in their families which "anchor" their racial identities. Mixed-race identities would be an unsettling disturbance to this kind of human identity structure. If people were allowed to identify as mixed based on just the four categories of black, white, Asian, and Indian, there would be at least fifteen different categories: all four groups combined, each of the four groups taken separately, black-Asian-Indian, black-white-Asian, black-white-Indian, white-Asian-Indian, black-white, Asian-white, Asian-Indian, Indian-white, black-Asian and black-Indian. The resulting mixed-race identities would also vary, depending on whether it was parents, grandparents, or great-grandparents who were members of the different races in mixed-race ancestry. There would be a multiplicity of possibilities for fractional identification and inclusive identification. Those people who wanted to be known as generically mixed might have to be recategorized according to the ways in which they were mixed, not to mention the task of specifying the racial composition of those who didn't want any racial identification at all. If you add to this the probability of change in individual racial identity over a lifetime, it's clear that the wide-scale social accommodation of mixed-race identity would make racial identity socially unintelligible. If racial identity were unintelligible, the remaining social barriers against interracial marriage would break down and the result would be even more racially mixed individuals and more confusion about identity and identification. There would be no way to tell the race of a person by looking at him or her. This *rhizomatic* nature of mixed-race identity, in contrast to the *rooted* nature of monoracial identity, is an unsettling prospect to many Americans. However, that it is unsettling, or upsetting, does not mean that it is morally wrong or that anyone has a right to control or stop it—assuming that it could be controlled or stopped.

A second set of objections to mixed-race identity comes from nonwhite concerns that categories of mixed race would decrease the numbers within minority groups entitled to special treatment on the basis of race. During the ***Harlem Renaissance*** in black American art and literature in the 1920s and 1930s, the light-skinned segment of the black population, known as the ***mulatto elite,*** gave up their mixed-race identity for the sake of Negro solidarity. This group had always had more money and education than the darker, less privileged majority of the black population; many were part of what Negro leaders called "The Talented Tenth." Some members of the mulatto elite could trace their ancestry back to white Southern aristocrats, and some of their families had been free for generations before the Emancipation Proclamation. (It is often overlooked that not all American blacks were enslaved during slavery, and that today, some American blacks are descended from immigrants who arrived after slavery or are themselves naturalized citizens.) Nevertheless, despite the white appearance of some members of the mulatto elite, and no matter their degree of education or cultural refinement, white society had never allowed them into its ranks. When the mulatto elite, as a group, came to terms with their exclusion from white society during the Harlem Renaissance, their affirmation of black identity was an important contribution to black solidarity.

To reintroduce mixed-race identity for mixed whites-and-blacks at this time in history could undermine the solidarity based on race that exists in the black population. It would suggest that blacks are no more than a ***social group*** that is externally constituted and would ignore the ways in which they are a ***social entity*** that has internal interactions.

As well, solidarity and loyalty based on race are important for American blacks and American Indians because whites have traditionally favored the lighter-skinned mixed-race members of both groups and externally appointed them as leaders of blacks and Indians in order to control the groups from within. That kind of external control can no longer be imposed on either group due to the emphasis placed on positive nonwhite identities since the 1960s. But discussion of mixed-race identity sometimes opens these old wounds of division, corruption, and manipulation.

However, mixed-race identity is different for American Indians than African Americans because acceptance as Indian by Indian groups is strongly dependent on cultural practices. Many contemporary American Indians do not appear to be Indian and may in fact have no Indian ancestry in the racial sense. Since 1970, American Indian identification has tripled from 827,000 to 2.2 million. The Cherokee Nation, which has doubled in membership to 182,000, has no "blood" requirement. What this difference amounts to is that for blacks, mixed-race identity represents leaving the group while for Indians, mixed-race identity represents joining the group.

Finally, the most radical argument against recognized mixed-race identities is that they would perpetuate scientifically unfounded classifications by race. *If race is unreal, then so is mixed race unreal.*

Traditional arguments against mixed-race identities, for the sake of preserving nonwhite identities (or protecting white identities, for that matter) generally presuppose the value of conformity to custom. They are not arguments based on moral principles or the value of individual rights. We will therefore conclude this chapter by considering ways in which the value of custom in racial issues might be criticized. Custom changes as historical circumstances change. The Civil Rights movement of the 1960s and 1970s was an historical change that was deliberately undertaken because it was morally wrong to practice racial discrimination and segregation in edu-cation, employment, housing, and public facilities. The recognition of mixed race for those people who want to be so recognized is simply a further development of the basic civil liberties defended in the Civil Rights movement. Each time a previously unrecognized social group achieves liberation, some people, especially those who benefited from the oppression of that group, are uncomfortable. This discomfort is the price of freedom.

The social confusion that could result from giving free play to all possible racial identities based on mixture might be nothing more than the undoing of the false bio-logical idea of race. Confusion is often a price of social change, but the first genera-tion growing up under the new system learns it from scratch in primary school, and by the time they teach it to their children, the confusion is no longer a problem. If we had all grown up without being taught about the three or four main racial groups in Amer-ica, we would not now be struggling with the problems caused by that false system of racial classification. Mixed-race identity may conflict with ideals based on (singular) roots, but maybe not everyone does or can hold such ideals. Perhaps the people with ideals of roots could continue to practice their traditions and also develop tolerance and respect for those who do not or cannot pursue the same ideals.

The objection that mixed-race identity would perpetuate classification by race fails to fully consider what most people mean by race or racial identity, namely, racial purity. Recognized mixed-race identity would undo the assumption that everyone is racially pure, and may, in the process, undo the assumption that everyone belongs to a race or that race is a meaningful way to type people.

D. DISCUSSION QUESTIONS

1. Is there any difference in principle between black-and-white racial mixture and other cases of racial mixture?

2. Do you think that mixed-race individuals have a right to identify as they choose? (Support your answer.)

3. Why do you think that mixed race has never been officially recognized in the United States?

4. Based on someone you know, imagine, or have read about, present a case study of being a mixed-race American.

5. If mixed-race people have the right to identify themselves racially, does this mean that anyone should have the right to racially identify any way at all? Give reasons either way.

E. RECOMMENDED READING

For the concept of universal human rights, see *The United Nations Charter: The Uni-versal Declaration of Human Rights.* Article 2 asserts universal rights of nondiscrim-ination; Article 20 (2) states, "No one may be compelled to belong to an association."

Historical information on mixed black-and-white race in the United States can be found in: John G. Mencke, *Mulattoes and Race Mixture: American Attitudes and Images, 1865–1918;* Paul Spickard, *Mixed Blood: Intermarriage and Ethnic Identity in Twentieth Century America;* Joel Williamson, *New People;* Naomi Zack, *Race and Mixed Race,* Part II. Sources on free blacks during slavery include: David W. Cohen and Jack P. Greene, eds., *Neither Slave nor Free: The Freedmen of African Descent in the Slave Societies of the New World;* Ira Berlin, *Slaves without Masters: The Free Negro in the Antebellum South.*

On contemporary mixed-race Americans, see L. Funderburg, *Black, White, Other: Biracial Americans Talk About Race and Identity.* See also Karya Gibel Azoulay, *Black, Jewish, and Interracial.*

On the possibilities for flexible mixed-race identity, see M. P. P. Root's "A Bill of Rights for Racially Mixed People," in Root, ed., *The Multiracial Experience: Racial Borders as the New Frontier;* in this volume see also Carlos A. Fernández, "La Raza and the Melting Pot." See Root's affirmation of nonwhite identities for mixed-race people in "The Multiracial Contribution to the Psychological Browning of America," in Naomi Zack, ed., *American Mixed Race: The Culture of Microdiversity.* For aracial mixed-race identity, see: Cecile Ann Lawrence, "Racelessness," and Naomi Zack, "Life After Race," in Zack, ed., *American Mixed Race.* Also in *American Mixed Race:* Linda Alcoff, in "Mestizo Identity," explores mixed-race Hispanic identities; Susan Graham, in "Grassroots Advocacy," and Carlos A. Fernández, in "Testimony of the Association of MultiEthnic Americans," favor adding a mixed-race category to the U.S. census; F. James Davis discusses mixed-race identity in Hawaii in "The Hawaiian Alternative to the One-Drop Rule." Zack offers philosophic justification for recognizing mixed race in "Mixed Black and White Race and Public Policy," in *Hypatia.*

Sources on mixed-race Native American categories include: Jack D. Forbes, *Black Africans and Native Americans: Color, Race and Caste in the Evolution of Red-Black Peoples;* David McCord and William Cleveland, *Black and Red: The Historical Meeting of Africans and Native Americans;* William J. Scheik, *The Half-Blood: A Cultural Symbol in 19th-Century American Fiction;* Mariella Squire-Hakey, "Yankee Imperialism and Imperialist Nostalgia," in Zack, ed., *American Mixed Race;* Terry P. Wilson, "Blood Quantum: Native American Mixed Bloods," in Maria P. P. Root, *Racially Mixed People in America.* The data on contemporary tribal membership can be found in *The Statistical Record of Native North Americans.*

David Theo Goldberg, in "Made in the USA," in Naomi Zack, ed., *American Mixed Race,* discusses some problems with mixed-race identity in the context of South Africa.

Y OUR MOTHER'S RELATIVES ARE TRADITIONAL AND THEY OBSERVE THE HOLIDAYS OF THEIR FOREBEARS. WHEN YOU ARE WITH THEM AT FAMILY GATHERINGS YOU SOMETIMES FEEL AS THOUGH YOU ARE IN A FOREIGN COUNTRY IN A DIFFERENT HISTORICAL PERIOD. BUT YOU STILL FIND THESE FAMILY GATHERINGS VERY SATISFYING BECAUSE YOU THINK THAT THEY ARE PART OF *WHAT YOU ARE* AND *WHERE YOU COME FROM.* WHY IS THAT IMPORTANT? YOUR FATHER'S RELATIVES SEEM TO BE TYPICAL, LATE TWENTIETH-CENTURY AMERICANS, WITH NO SPECIAL FAMILY CUSTOMS. IS THAT A FORM OF ETHNICITY, TOO?

CHAPTER 4

ETHNICITY

INTRODUCTION

Ethnicity is a characteristic of distinct groups that may or may not be geographically united and that can be identified both across and within nations. For example, Jews, as an ethnic group, have always been dispersed among different nations throughout their history, constituting a *diaspora;* by contrast, the Lapps in Finland have remained in the same geographical area over many centuries. At this time in human history, there are very few ethnic groups that have no members who have left their ancestral homelands.

Generally speaking, ethnicity concerns all the aspects of daily, family, and cultural life that people with common histories share and find obligatory and fulfilling to teach to their children. In popular thought, ethnicity is a matter of learned behavior with variable connections to biological heredity. Although, as something passed on to people by families and communities, ethnicity is inherited, it differs from race. Few Americans now believe that ethnicity is biologically or genetically inherited in ways that would develop in individuals if they grew up separated from their families or ethnic communities.

In the United States, members of the same ethnic groups tend to be of the same race: Irish, German, Italian, French, English, and Polish Americans are white ethnic groups; Sioux, Mohawk, Pueblo, and Iroquois Indian nations are viewed as different ethnic groups in the same racial category; and Japanese, Chinese, Vietnamese, and Koreans are seen, by whites at least, as ethnic types of Asians. However, the model of ethnicity as a simple subcategory of race has important exceptions: Hispanics are a racially variable ethnic group; most Jews are now considered white but some are black; Native Americans vary racially as well as ethnically; and there are nonwhite members of every European nationality. Many Americans who are *monoracial* are *multiethnic.* Mixed-race individuals are sometimes multiethnic and sometimes monoethnic. Indeed, the fluidity and mixture of ethnicities in the United States is so widespread and commonly accepted that the terms monoethnic and multiethnic are not needed.

Beyond the loose association of ethnicity with culture as opposed to biology, it is difficult to say anything further about ethnicity in general. Some ethnic groups have similar physical appearances among members; others do not. Most ethnic groups share common languages but many do not. Some ethnic groups have strong traditions of solidarity and community while others are more divided. And so on. Ethnicity, in contrast to race and nationality, is very difficult to account for with generalities. This particularity of ethnicity makes it resistant to any **grand theory.** Instead, the study of ethnicity is a **narrative** discipline, made up of the stories of interlocking groups.

In some parts of the world, ethnic differences are the basis of bloodshed and oppression that has gone on for centuries. In the United States, ethnicity and ethnic difference have been tamed in ways that presently appear to allow for tolerance and harmony. For this reason, the word *ethnicity* is often used as a euphemism for race when speakers want to refer to race without causing offense to diverse listeners or drawing anger upon themselves. Thus, racial differences, in the sense of false biological differences, may be referred to as "ethnic differences," or reference may be made to an individual's or group's "ethnicity" when what is meant is their race in the false biological sense. The reason that *ethnicity* is less charged than *race* is that in the United States, unlike many other parts of the world, ethnic differences have not been as important as racial differences as a continuous ground for prejudice, oppression, or exclusion from the social goods controlled by dominant groups.

In this chapter we will explore the meaning of ethnicity in comparison to race. Section A is a theoretical discussion of how what people think of as race really is nothing more than ethnicity. Section B presents some of the historical developments of ethnicity as an American form of human categories and **identity.** Section C is an open-ended discussion, through example, of the ethnic complexity in contemporary American life.

A. RACE AS ETHNICITY

Race does not have the biological foundation it is assumed to have and ethnicity is no longer assumed to have a fixed biological foundation in the social or physical sciences. Thus race is nothing more, and nothing less, than ethnicity. That is, the main nonwhite racial groups that are recognized in American society do not each have biological essences or distinct collections of physical traits that distinguish them from one another. What their members do share are varied degrees of common geographical ancestry, common histories of oppression in the United States, common goals of liberation, and perhaps common stereotypes. It is this kind of common culture that is valued by Indians, Asians, and African Americans. Indeed, it would probably be the main reason that many nonwhites would be reluctant to abandon their racial classification even after a thorough analysis of the false biological foundation of racial classification (see Chapter 1).

An awareness of shared culture and identity among members of a racial group, together with interactions among members of that group that do not take place with members of other groups, make racial groups *social entities* in the same way that ethnic groups are social entities. The cohesive aspects of racial belonging are in principle no different from aspects of ethnic belonging. Criteria for recognized racial group membership tend to be based on physical appearance that includes skin color, hair texture, and bone structure, as well as ways of speaking, dressing, and moving, and styles of behavior. While black and white Americans associate such criteria for group membership with belonging to a race in the false biological sense, there is little in such criteria that differs from criteria for ethnic group membership. This is especially true when members of the same ethnic group are expected to have a common appearance. That is, since race is biologically unreal, its social reality *reduces* to ethnicity. In popular thought, however, the cultural aspects of ethnicity often are first divided from what are believed to be biological aspects of race. The cultures or ethnicities of different races are then falsely assumed to be biologically inherited. This assumption that ethnicity is inherited through race is a remnant of nineteenth-century theories of race that posited racial essences as the vehicle or medium for inherited cultural and behavioral traits, such as aptitudes or talents.

Once the model of race became restricted to biological traits only, the link between racial biological traits and cultural traits and behavior was broken. Without the link to biological heredity, the American notion of ethnicity as cultural inheritance seems to permit support of, and respect for, difference, without the kinds of human distancing that accompany the old biologically essentialist ideas of race. Although members of the same ethnic group may share some traits of physical appearance due to real biological family inheritance, as things now stand, few people believe that they are making racial statements when they say that an individual looks Irish, doesn't look Italian, could be German, or would not be taken for Jewish. People who make such statements are probably unable to explain what they mean by them beyond reference to their past experience of the appearance of people whose ethnicities were known to them. Because the projection of racial differences, in the false sense of biological essences, onto differences in human appearance has no foundation in science and causes many social and individual problems, the question is: Why not *reconfigure* race as ethnicity?

The reconfiguration of race as ethnicity is at this point a theoretical possibility. It would be difficult to accomplish in social reality, mainly due to historical ways in which the success of diverse white European ethnic groups in America has been tied to their gradual identification as racially white. Because the white racial group has always been the most successful group socially, economically, and politically, many whites might see the reconfiguration of blacks, Asians, and Indians as ethnic groups, rather than racial groups, as an assault on their own privileged identity as white. By the same token, blacks, Asians, and Indians who still feel aggrieved at past oppression and believe they are still victimized by racism would be wary of such a reconfiguration. From a nonwhite perspective, the danger of changing race to ethnicity in popular consciousness is that whites would still make judgments based on the false ideas of race that would systematically favor those who used to be called white over those who used to be called black, Asian, Indian, mixed, and so forth. If the same judgments and discriminations were still made in the absence of explicit categories of race, the nonwhite racial groups once reconfigured as ethnic groups would have no recognized grounds on which to seek social justice. The reconfiguration of race into ethnicity would thus be an *eliminative* development of ideas of race that would entail the general problems with eliminativism discussed in Chapter 2.

B. HISTORICAL DEVELOPMENTS OF AMERICAN ETHNICITY

Before culture or ethnicity was conceptually separated from race in the biological sense, early twentieth-century sociologists posited as many different races as would be considered ethnic groups today. Until about 1920, Irish, Germans, Poles, Italians, and other non-northern and non-English European groups were studied as distinct races by social scientists. Jews were also considered to be a distinct race through World War II, especially by the Nazis, who used racist anti-Semitic propaganda to motivate and justify the persecution and attempted genocide of European Jews. This racialization of Jews came to be seen as an integral part of anti-Semitism, and few Americans now consider Irish, Germans, Poles, or other non-northern Europeans to be distinct races. Yet racial categories based on non-European ancestry such as Africa, Asia, and even the Americas, still stand.

In the United States, from colonial days onward, the dominant economic and social class has been English, Scandinavian, and German in national origin. And in this predominantly Christian country, Protestantism has been the dominant religion (though there are many different branches or sects of Protestantism). Late nineteenth-century and early twentieth-century European immigrants who were Catholic faced the task of assimilating to the cultural behavior of the dominant Protestant, northern European ruling class as part of the process of becoming American; the same held true for Jews, especially those from Eastern Europe because they did not belong to preferred immigrant nationalities. During the same time, two main models of American national cohesion were in contention. There was the *melting pot* model whereby different ethnic groups would intermarry and share their cultural traditions, resulting in a new American blend. The second model was *pluralism.* According to the early model of pluralism, all citizens would maintain private personal and family ethnic traditions while participating as ethnically neutral Americans in public and civic life. A later model of pluralism, which is more persuasive today, entails that different ethnic groups bring their distinct cultural identities into their roles in public and civic life.

During the second half of the twentieth century, the culture presented as American through the mass media, as well as the cultural styles that dominate in the upper echelons of business, politics, and higher education, have been represented as *ethnically neutral.* Foods, music, and personal styles from distinct ethnicities have been incorporated into images and products for popular consumption. However, these nationally consumed items of ethnic diversity are usually more bland than their "prototypes" in ethnicities of origin. Still, it is important to note that the mass-market appropriation and distribution of such material and cultural products displays little discrimination on the grounds of ethnicity or, for that matter, race or social class. All cultural modes are associated with consumer products through advertising because they help sell those products. The slang, music, artwork, fashion, and hairstyles of the most disadvantaged and otherwise despised subgroups, such as prisoners, drug dealers, gangsters, lesbians, and gay men, are publicly displayed and personally imitated by members of dominant groups, especially teenagers and young adults—all without apparent prejudice.

But despite ethnic neutrality in the mainstream and perhaps true egalitarianism in lifestyle accessories, it is not clear to what extent the United States is ethnically neutral at the close of the twentieth century. Ethnically diverse European groups have been able to assimilate as they have risen socioeconomically and sent their children to college. It is not obvious whether this means that the successful mainstream of American culture is ethnically neutral or whether its new members continually acquire the dominant **WASP** (white, Anglo-Saxon Protestant) culture. Some contemporary critics insist that what appears to be ethnic neutrality is in fact a blend of northern European cultures. On this view, the successful assimilation of American European ethnic groups requires exchanging their distinct ethnicities for the ethnicity of the dominant ethnic groups. In other words, Italian, Irish, Jewish, and even some Asian and black Americans who have joined the mainstream have done so by becoming a different ethnicity, at least in their work or student identities. But, the success and assimilation of Jews and Asians often results in new expressions of anti-Semitism and racism against them, precisely on account of their assimilation and success in comparison with other minorities. This suggests that the American elite is still expected to be WASP, an expectation that could be a reflex of tradition, a facet of ongoing anti-Semitism and racism, or both.

We should consider that although the dominant ethnicity of American elites may be northern European, it is hardly a replica of ethnicities in northern Europe, but rather, something new. In fact, the desirability of American consumer products is viewed as a threat to tradition in northern Europe as much as in the Third World. English is the official language in the United States but it is spoken in a version that has become distinctly American. American high culture—art, music, literature, architecture—is different from that of every other country in the world; American popular culture—music, movies, television, fast food—is even more distinctive and more in demand internationally.

Finally, one might take the view that the United States, in comparison with most other countries, is still a young nation. American ethnicity, as a distinct way of living that Americans feel obligated and find fulfilling to teach their children, is still being formed. The continual change in this work-in-progress obscures the ways in which American ethnicity is automatically accepted and passed on by most Americans.

When people from non-northern European ethnic groups, Asians, and African Americans become part of the mainstream, they not only change their own ethnicities but subtly change the ethnic qualities of the mainstream. This raises the question, Why should the "mainstream" values and styles of the social, economic, political, and educational elites be viewed as definitive of ethnicity in America? Perhaps the ethnicity of those on the bottom and margins of society—those who are poor and un-dereducated; those whose lives take alternative forms due to disabilities, special tal-ents, nontraditional family structures; those who are not heterosexual, who are in prison, illiterate, here illegally, have AIDS, or are homeless—perhaps they and their ethnic groups are as definitive of a distinct American ethnicity as members of the mainstream. That is, perhaps American ethnicity resembles neither the puree of a melting pot nor the stew of pluralism with identifiable ingredients. Instead, it may be made up of so many changing side dishes that choices consist of extreme specializa-tion and unpredictable combinations. Perhaps all we can say about American ethnic-ity is that it has so many different elements and types that it can be studied only through direct experience or in works of history, literature, and film that record spe-cific events in the lives of particular individuals and groups. It may simply elude sys-tematic theory or generalization.

C. CONTEMPORARY ETHNIC DIVERSITY

Americans have always been self-consciously diverse ethnically, even though En-glish and northern European ancestries have predominated among elites. Along with this diversity, other cultural factors have undermined distinct ethnic identities. Eth-nicity does not exist on its own but in reality *intersects* both with race and religion in varied ways: blacks and whites are ethnically different due to different cultural expe-rience associated with racial difference; Jews, Catholics, and Protestants have differ-ent traditions of social and family life; all religious affiliations occur among blacks, whites, Asians, and American Indians.

Dominant ethnic groups are also dominant socioeconomic groups, and people often change or revise their ethnicities as they rise socioeconomically. This suggests that ethnic life in the United States is dependent on nonethnic factors, such as money and political power. The technological, capitalistic, consumer-based society in which we function does not have a primary goal of preserving lifestyles that derive from foreign countries of ancestral origin. The economically driven aspects of American cultural life are not so much neutral in terms of ethnic preference as they are *non-ethnic.* Ethnically distinctive lifestyles have been further undermined by extensive intermarriage among white European ethnic groups, by the breakdown of extended families, and by high rates of divorce in nuclear families. As a result, many Ameri-cans do not feel "ethnic" at all.

However, socioeconomic factors reinforce the ethnic identities of those who are not successful, especially when ethnicity is connected to race. The ways in which race intersects with social class will be discussed in Chapters 7 and 11. As a general rule, we can note here that degrees of ethnicity vary inversely with socioeconomic status. Among nonwhites and eastern and southern European ethnic groups, as pov-erty and disenfranchisement increase, so do ethnic visibility and internal senses of ethnic identity.

Nevertheless, on all socioeconomic levels, many Americans still identify in terms of their ethnic ancestry. Ethnic differences can spark intense conflicts between groups, especially when combined with perceived racial differences. Consider, for example, debates about whether English is to be the only language taught or used to teach in primary schools with students from Hispanic immigrant families who have not been taught English at home. Or try to construct a reasonable position on the question of whether *Ebonics,* the language composed of current slang and traditional black speech, ought to be used to teach black schoolchildren who can easily express themselves in Ebonics but do not have well-developed skills in standard English. If urban neighborhoods with dominant populations of Asian immigrants have shop signs in Korean and Chinese, should public service information such as traffic signs be provided in these languages as well as English? Are the benefits from multilingual public speech worth the sacrifice of unity through the imposition of one language? Or is the real issue one of dominance rather than unity? If standard American English is continually enforced as the national language, is this unjustly destructive of immigrant and racial ethnicities?

Suppose that English is the standard American language solely because English speakers have always been the most politically powerful group in the United States. If a wide range of linguistic diversity were publicly represented, many Americans who speak only English might need to become multilingual. However, Americans have a tradition of not wanting to learn "foreign languages." Is it right to "force" Americans to learn foreign languages?

Language aside, the nondominant ethnicities in the United States lack histories of harmonious intergroup relationships. Rivalries between Italian and Irish Catholics, Cubans and Puerto Ricans, Japanese and Chinese, black Africans and American blacks, and Orthodox and Reform Jews are well-known examples. In recent decades, bitter, racially motivated disputes between American Jews and African Americans have occurred in public forums.

From the turn of the century until the 1970s, American Jews were major supporters of black attempts to secure civil rights and economic and social advancement. American anti-Semites had traditionally excluded Jews from high public office, university and professional employment, and "polite" society. American Jews were also aware of their history of persecution and brutal oppression in almost every European country. Knowledge of this past suffering was reason for Jews to empathize with the struggles of American blacks who had been victims of slavery, segregation, lynching and other forms of violence, and were denied public social amenities and excluded from higher education and professional employment. More than this, many American Jews were intellectually and morally aware that racial injustice violated democratic principles. Many of the activists who led integration and voter registration efforts in the South during the Civil Rights movement were Jewish. During the 1950s and 1960s, Jewish philanthropists helped fund social justice projects supporting blacks, and Jewish liberals voted for politicians who were committed to programs supporting black advancement from what was called "second-class citizenship."

But by the late 1960s, part of the American black leadership was advocating *separatism* and retaliatory violence against whites as strategies of *Black Power.* This leadership also urged American black solidarity with other groups in the African diaspora throughout the world. For example, support was expressed for Palestinians who viewed Israeli military action against them as racist.

While few American Jews have been *Zionists,* most have considered support of Israel to be an important part of their Jewish identity. By the early 1970s, insofar as Jews identified with both white Americans and Israel, there was a broad withdrawal of

Jewish interest from black social problems. As well, some Jewish Americans became *neoconservatives* during the 1970s and 1980s. Due to new economic and political concerns, they no longer voted for the government-funded social welfare programs that assisted blacks. Black extremist ideologues countered by resurrecting old European and Nazi myths of Jewish financial conspiracies and exploitation of oppressed groups.

Contemporary black-Jewish conflict is driven by economic and political interests that have become symbolized by ethnic difference. The antagonists perceive their ethnic differences to be racial differences, and each side expresses itself as morally superior to the other. Neither side benefits. American Jews are a small minority that has only recently been successful in the mainstream. They cannot plausibly be held responsible for all or most of the problems experienced by American blacks. Blacks have endured severe economic, political, and social problems and they do not have a history of persecuting any other group. American antiblack racism is more extensive than Jewish antiblack politics, and American anti-Semitism is more extensive than black anti-Semitism. When Jews attack blacks on racial grounds or blacks attack Jews, both draw on the ideologies of historical oppressors who were neither black nor Jewish. Also, white American anti-Semitism is still part of the "platform" of white supremacy, and it is not definite that the present success and apparent acceptance of Jews in the American mainstream represents a permanent eradication of anti-Semitism among the ruling elites of the United States.

D. DISCUSSION QUESTIONS

1. Which of these questions do you think most Americans would be more comfortable in answering, and why: What is your race? What is your ethnicity?

2. Why do you think that ethnic difference is less of a problem in the United States than racial difference?

3. Is there a favored American ethnicity? Describe it or explain why it does not exist.

4. What problems, if any, are faced by Americans whose parents are from different ethnic groups? Provide an example from your own experience.

5. Would a raceless society have to be a society without ethnic diversity?

E. RECOMMENDED READING

Source material on specific ethnic groups in American history includes: James Paul Allen and Eugene James Turner, *We The People: An Atlas of America's Ethnic Diversity;* Leonard Dinnerstein, Roger L. Nichols, and David M. Reimers, eds., *Natives and Strangers: A Multicultural History of Americans;* Maldwyn Allen Jones, *American Immigration;* Stephen Thernstrom, ed., *Harvard Encyclopedia of American Ethnic Groups.*

For a history of American social science and ethnicity, see R. Fred Wacker, *Ethnicity, Pluralism and Race.* For political science and literary perspectives on

American ethnic difference (respectively), see Michael Walzer, "Pluralism: A Political Perspective," in Will Kymlicka, ed., *The Rights of Minority Cultures,* and Walter Benn Michaels, *Our America: Nativism, Modernism and Pluralism.* See also, Milton M. Gordon's *Assimilation in American Life.*

Contemporary critical work on ethnicity includes: Homi Bhabha, *The Location of Culture;* Claudia Card, "Race, Racism, and Ethnicity," in Linda Bell and David Blumenfeld, eds., *Overcoming Sexism and Racism;* Linda Chavez, *Out of the Barrio: Toward a New Politics of Hispanic Assimilation;* J. Angelo Corlett, "Parallels of Ethnicity and Gender," in Naomi Zack, ed., *RACE/SEX;* Steven Steinberg, *The Ethnic Myth.* On literary concerns arising out of belonging to more than one culture, see John C. Hawley, ed., *Cross-Addressing: Resistance Literature and Cultural Borders.*

For narrative accounts of American ethnicity, see: Julia Alvarez, *How the Garcia Girls Lost Their Accents;* Harold Augenbraum and Ilan Stavans, eds., *Growing up Latino;* Raymond A. Beliotti, *Seeking Identity;* Marilyn P. Davis, *Mexican Voices/ American Dreams;* Nazli Kibria, "Migration and Vietnamese American Women: Remaking Ethnicity," in Maxine Baca Zinn and Bonnie Thornton Dill, eds., *Women of Color in U.S. Society.* A primary source on militant black ethnicity and its problems is Louis Farrakhan, "Interview in *National Alliance* Newspaper," in William Pleasant, ed., *Independent Black Leadership in America.*

On American Jewish ethnicity and identity, see: David Theo Goldberg and Michael Krausz, eds., *Jewish Identity.* A classic literary source is Henry Roth's novel, *Call It Sleep.* Analyses of black-Jewish conflict are presented in Cornel West, *Race Matters,* chapter 6, and Naomi Zack, "On Being and Not-Being Black and Jewish," in Maria P. P. Root, ed., *The Multiracial Experience: Racial Borders as the New Frontier.*

Y OU ARE NOT A RACIST. A CLOSE FRIEND OF YOURS WHO
BELONGS TO THE SAME RACE YOU DO OFTEN MAKES HATEFUL
AND HURTFUL REMARKS ABOUT MEMBERS OF A DIFFERENT RACIAL
GROUP. YOU HAVE TRIED TO REASON WITH YOUR FRIEND AND HAVE
MADE IT CLEAR THAT YOU DO NOT SHARE HER OPINIONS, BUT IT
HASN'T CHANGED HER BEHAVIOR. YOU HAVE KNOWN HER SINCE
JUNIOR HIGH SCHOOL AND HAVE SHARED MANY IMPORTANT EVENTS
OF YOUR LIFE WITH HER, SO IT WOULDN'T OCCUR TO YOU TO END THE
FRIENDSHIP. IS THERE ANYTHING THAT YOU ARE MORALLY *OBLIGATED*
TO DO CONCERNING HER RACISM?

CHAPTER 5

RACISM

INTRODUCTION

The word *racism* is relatively new. When the hierarchical paradigm of race was accepted in popular culture, *"n"egroes*—the word was spelled with a small *n* until the
1930s—were believed to be genetically inferior to whites culturally, aesthetically, intellectually, and morally. During that time, *discrimination* against Negroes for jobs,
education, housing, and within the criminal justice system was neither illegal nor
considered by most whites to be morally wrong. The same held true for racial discrimination against Native Americans and Asians; it was not illegal, and few whites
thought it was immoral. It's easy to forget that the word *discrimination* is an under-
statement of conditions that included the enslavement, rape, lynching, beating, murder, unjust imprisonment, and humiliation of American blacks by whites that went on
for hundreds of years. Neither does the word discrimination connote the full reality
of the massacre of Indians and their expulsion from ancestral lands, or the exploitation of Asian American laborers in railroad construction and agriculture in the West
during the late nineteenth century. The physical *segregation* by race in housing, employment, and public facilities for American nonwhites after the Civil War reflected
those oppressive actions. That is, those who were mistreated were also separated and
excluded. Altogether, whites and nonwhites have lived radically different lives in this
country. The situation began to change in the 1960s, but most nonwhites are probably still aware of deep social differences based on race.

In the 1950s, the possibility of *integration* between blacks and whites became
a topic of national controversy. Integrationists viewed the differences between races
as a result of the disadvantages of nonwhites, especially in education, that were kept

in place by white ***bigotry.*** Segregation in schools, workplaces, and public facilities was defended by white Southerners on the grounds that integration would result in ***miscegenation,*** mixed-race offspring from interracial marriage and sex. Popular fears about this threat to ***white purity*** were based on what would today be called the old racist theory of the hierarchy of the races.

During the 1950s, a distinction was made between ***de facto*** segregation that existed unintended and ***de jure*** segregation that was legislated. When the Supreme Court ruled in *Brown v. Board of Education* that public schools had to be integrated, both forms of segregation were struck down in principle. However, it took decades to counteract the will of many white communities to segregate and de facto segregation still exists throughout American primary education and in housing.

After civil rights were legally secured for blacks in the mid-1960s, American blacks began calling themselves *"blacks"* and *"Afro-Americans"* instead of "Negroes." The change in preferred designation reflected a resurgence of pride in being black, based on African origins. It was accompanied by renewed commitment to social self-sufficiency within the black community and new goals for economic and educational advancement. During this period, the concept of racism developed. Racism came to be considered a moral and social evil on the grounds that people of different races are equal in human potential and that it is morally wrong to harm others solely because they are racially different from those doing the harm. It is important to note here that even if people of different races were not equal in human potential, it would still be morally wrong to harm them on the basis of racial difference, for the following reasons: Human beings are not responsible for those traits they have that others consider to be racial traits. People ought not to be harmed (or blamed or insulted) for things for which they are not responsible.

Both a denial of the premise of equal human potential across race and advocacy of harm based on racial difference have come to be considered racist positions. Direct harm is easy to identify because it consists of insult, assault, and murder by private citizens and unjust treatment by police, juries, judges, and lawmakers. Indirect harm through denial of opportunity to better one's situation in life and of earned rewards, is more difficult to recognize by those who are not victims of it. The question of where to draw the line between harm that ought to be a matter of private and public morality and harm that ought to be legislated against is a subject of continued disagreement. For example, Americans agree that there ought to be equal opportunity in education for children of all races, but disagree on what measures government ought to take to implement this. When school integration requires busing or administrative authority over parental choice, many who otherwise endorse equality claim that its implementation violates their liberty.

The debate about whether ***hate speech*** ought to be punished on account of the ***offense*** it causes also turns on disagreement about the comparative values of equality and liberty. Some critics have argued that although the censorship of hate speech may curtail racism, it also curtails the right to free speech. The violation of free speech rights that are protected by the First Amendment to the U.S. Constitution is thus held to be a greater social and individual harm than the harm caused by hate speech. However, those who defend laws and penalties against hate speech have argued that its potential to offend and even cause trauma in contexts where it is intended to do those very things means that it should be considered not speech, but action. On this view, hate speech is a broader category than what used to be known as *fighting words,* language that immediately and directly provokes or incites violence. The censorship of hate speech as a form of action would be justified on the principle that actions which harm others are not protected by law. Rather, the rights to life and liberty of the victims of such actions are protected by laws against murder, assault, battery, and the like.

Suppose that hate speech is considered a form of action. Because any speech can be hateful under the right circumstances, in principle, all speech then qualifies as a form of action. The right to free speech was originally secured to create an area of freedom for individual expression where such expression did not in itself directly harm others. In the liberal democratic tradition, the range of freedom in speech has always been more broad than the range of freedom in action, simply because most people recognize that speech is not action. Some defenders of First Amendment rights have argued that the designation of hate speech as action would blur the important distinction between speech and action. Without that distinction, all forms of protected individual expression would be jeopardized.

Even if hate speech were a form of action, what distinguishes it from other forms of action is its offensive nature. However, it is not obvious that people have a *positive right* to be legally protected from being offended by others, or even a *negative right* that others not offend them. Conservatives as well as liberals, whites as well as blacks, and heterosexuals as well as homosexuals find many things offensive that others consider it part of their liberty to express or do. It would therefore be a dangerous restriction of everyone's liberty to outlaw hate speech because it is offensive. Of course, this does not mean that hate speech ought not to be condemned according to social rules and moral judgment.

Regardless of exactly where they stand on free speech issues, most Americans today believe that racism is morally wrong. However, whites and nonwhites differ on the amount and extent of racism that they believe exists in American society at this time. Few whites who are not *white supremacists* would identify themselves as racists, and most whites are very indignant at the accusation or implication that their beliefs or actions are racist. Many nonwhites believe that racism against nonwhites, especially blacks, is still widespread and powerful in American life. For that reason, they often do not understand why whites are troubled and distressed when they are called racists, or why whites think that to have their beliefs or actions called racist is to be accused of an unusual moral crime. The purpose of this chapter is to clarify the contemporary concept of racism. Section A is a discussion of *classic racism.* Section B is a discussion of *unintentional* and *institutional racism.* Section C considers the question of whether nonwhites can be racist.

A. CLASSIC RACISM

The meaning or concept of racism for the majority of white Americans refers to hatred, hostility, contempt and harmful intentions in individuals' hearts and minds. According to this definition, a racist is someone who has ill will toward other races and expresses that ill will in speech and action, through racial slurs, insults based on race, unfair behavior based on race and unprovoked violent behavior based on the race of victims. Racists in this classic sense would include Ku Klux Klan members, Nazis and neo-Nazis, and anyone else who—whether acting alone or as a member of a group—advocates harming people of other races. Classic racism is thus conscious and deliberate.

Classic racism occurs on a continuum. Some racists may never speak their true thoughts and feelings, others may express themselves only to close friends and relatives, and still others may act on their racism in whatever ways their daily lives afford. Classic racism is not at present socially acceptable in white middle-class society, either privately or publicly. Therefore, many contemporary classic racists are **covert.** They either deceive themselves or are discreet, secretive, and subtle about how they harm people of other races. There are two ways to look at this covert strain of classic racism: it's worse than **overt** classic racism because it is hidden and therefore difficult to confront directly with complete and accurate descriptions of what the classic racist thinks, feels, and does; it's not as harmful as overt classic racism because the need for concealment reinforces the public moral position that racism is wrong.

The number or percentage of white Americans who are classic racists is an empirical matter, difficult to measure. However, the charge or accusation of being a racist usually has the connotation of being a racist in this classic way. That is the sense in which most white Americans now consider it a serious insult, bordering on slander, to be called racists.

Classic racism victimizes nonwhites and is a serious moral vice in its own right according to broadly accepted public morality in most parts of this country. Strong attempts have been made to understand its causes and design remedies for it. Emotional and intellectual causes of noncriminal instances of classic racism have been sought, while criminal instances of it are legally punishable, based on harm done and intent to harm that can be proved.

The probable emotional causes of classic racism vary: compensation for feelings of inadequacy; displacement of anger at persons who are feared onto those who are believed to be vulnerable; projection of one's own shortcomings onto others; cruelty or sadism. Understanding racism as a form of compensation, displacement, or projection requires investigating prior harm experienced by the racist. However, cruelty or sadism are psychological distortions that may not always be understandable as reactions to harm experienced by racists, because some people are cruel or sadistic by temperament just as others may be kind or masochistic by temperament.

The main problem with explanations of racism in emotional terms is that they lack a moral dimension. Victims of racism might be understood to have matching emotional distortions, such as low self-esteem, guilt, or a (possibly unconscious) desire to experience shame, pain, and abuse. Such psychological interpretation is problematic because it imputes pathology to victims in ways that mitigate the injustice of classical racism, especially when its expressions are unexpected or when the victims are children. If racists are judged to be emotionally disturbed simply because they are racists, this lifts their moral responsibility for harm done. People who are not racists tend to hold racists responsible for the harm they do, whereas psychologically disturbed people may not be fully responsible for their mental states and resulting actions. If racists are not responsible for being racists, due to emotional disturbance, then they ought not to be blamed and punished for their racism and its effects.

The appropriate remedies for racism that is judged to be a form of emotional disturbance based on previous suffering or abuse would be to heal the racist and restore his or her self-love and self-esteem so that racism would not be necessary as a form of compensation or reaction. Such remedies would have to be applied in ways similar to other forms of psychotherapy. At this time, there are few, if any, systematic programs of psychological therapy for classic racists. Most nonracists consider racism a moral defect, both blameworthy and punishable. People are responsible for their moral defects because it is presumed to have been within their power not to develop them, or to correct them. Therefore, most nonracists do not advocate therapeutic approaches to racism. And most racists do not consider their racism to be an emotional illness, so they are unlikely to seek such help.

Cognitive psychological explanations of classic racism base it on ignorance. Perhaps classic racists don't know that the objects of their ill will are undeserving of such judgments and actions; perhaps classic racists are unaware of the harm they cause. The explanation of classic racism in terms of ignorance has structured the traditional educational model for remedying it. On this model, adult classic racists have been poorly taught about human difference and have failed to learn that skin color and other characteristics they associate with racial difference do not have the importance necessary to motivate and justify racist feelings and behavior. Classic racists may be intellectually trapped in a nineteenth-century view of the world that falsely divides human beings into distinct racial hierarchies. They may have a problem with standards for evidence in that they *overgeneralize* from encounters with a few members of a racial group. Such *intellectual errors* of *anachronism* or overgeneralization could result from an unreflective acceptance of views held by parents, neighbors, or peers. Both types of error would be reinforced by limited experience in interacting with people of different races.

On this cognitive model, the remedies for racism are information and education. Classic racists first need to be made aware of facts about people of different races. If this doesn't change their mistaken views, bad habits in reasoning have to be corrected. There has been considerable effort expended throughout the American educational system on such intellectual remedies. Observers differ on the success of teaching primary school, secondary school, and college students ideals and rules of nondiscrimination and racial egalitarianism, as a strategy for eliminating racism in the culture.

The endurance of classical racism in the United States has led some critics to speculate that racism may be a specific instance of a general human characteristic to respond to difference with hostility. It may be that a certain proportion of the population will always hate and try to harm members of groups different from the groups on which they base their own identity, whether the difference is in ethnicity, race, religion, sexual preference, geographical location, whatever. Short of outright hate, some people may always feel they have to compete with others on the basis of their group identity. If those are facts about human nature, then so long as racial difference is generally recognized, there will be classic racists.

Nonetheless, most nonracists view racism as a moral defect. The racist is someone who lacks basic *moral* or *ethical* impulses to *identify* with other living beings.

Such identification in the form of empathy or compassion, rests on the ability to seriously imagine oneself in the place of another. Those who can identify with others realize that being the object of racism is a painful experience. Because pain is intrinsically bad, it is wrong to cause pain in others without justification. Racial difference is not a justification for inflicting pain because people cannot help what race they are. We should blame and punish others only for things that they have done when they could have done otherwise. To hate or harm others on the grounds of race is unfair. This lack of fairness is a moral defect. Those who are fair and who are committed to behaving morally therefore have an obligation not only to continue to behave fairly themselves, but to react negatively to the unfairness of others. It is interesting to note that of all the perspectives on classic racism, only the moral view places a clear obligation on nonracists, as well as racists, to curtail racist speech and behavior.

B. UNINTENTIONAL AND INSTITUTIONAL RACISM

Pernicious and morally repugnant though classic racism is, it is only a small part—and perhaps not the most important part—of what scholars and social critics now mean by the word racism. The concept of *unintentional racism* differs from classic racism in that it is defined by the harmful-consequence side of speech and action, rather than by the kinds of motives and intentions that classic racists know they have. Nonwhites may be harmed without those who harm them intending to harm them on racial grounds, or sometimes without intent to harm them in any way. For example, a law-abiding pair of black teenagers may be psychologically harmed when elderly white adults cross the street to avoid them. The same pair may be further injured, this time physically, when they are arrested for a crime they did not commit because police officers think that the crime was committed by black teenagers, and those two happened to be in the area. Or, in another example, Mexican workers may be continually passed over for promotion in a company that has always filled its managerial jobs with whites.

The intention of elderly strollers might be physical safety, that of police officers, public safety, and upper management might be interested in securing competent middle management. Nonetheless, the common effect of these actions is a type of harm to nonwhites that many contemporary Americans, especially nonwhites, would call racist. This type of harm is called racist because it is suffered by nonwhites and not by whites.

Usually, acts of unintentional racism follow from derogatory assumptions about all members of nonwhite groups. The remedy for this type of racism has been to correct unsubstantiated generalizations and educate unintentional racists toward a realization of how their actions harm nonwhites. This remedy is based on the assumption that unintentional racists would not want to harm nonwhites unfairly.

Institutional racism is a characteristic of public, social, political, and economic organizations and traditions that are harmful to nonwhites. Those who carry out the practices of institutional racism may or may not be classic racists. Some institutional racism is overt, explicitly directed against targeted groups, while other forms of it are covert so that the harm is evident only after the fact. Examples of overt institutional racism are segregated public facilities before the Civil Rights Act of 1964 and the state laws prohibiting interracial marriage that existed before the U.S. Supreme Court struck them all down in 1967. Examples of covert institutional racism are requirements for participation that nonwhites cannot fill as easily as whites and attitudes held or actions taken on the basis of socially undesirable characteristics that occur more frequently among nonwhites than whites (such as poverty). Also, whites may be privileged due to having more social assets than nonwhites (such as college-educated relatives).

Overt, explicit institutional racism is, obviously, intentional racism. But much institutional racism in the United States at this time is not intentional. If blacks and Hispanics live in inner-city impoverished neighborhoods and their children thereby receive inferior social services compared to white children who live in the suburbs, the resulting institutional racism against nonwhite children is not necessarily intended. In a field where job promotion depends on social contact outside the workplace, if a community is socially segregated by race, nonwhites may fail to be promoted, even though their supervisors have no racist policies or intentions. In a job situation where whites have always occupied upper-level positions and nonwhites, lower ones, tradition alone works against nonwhites in ways that whites may not intend.

A status quo of nonwhite exclusion or underrepresentation tends to be accepted as "normal" in such situations, and most people have to make a special effort in order to change what is normal. While it could be argued that most of the examples of institutional racism cited thus far do not directly harm nonwhites, they do harm them indirectly by restricting their opportunities for employment and economic advancement. The restriction of those opportunities leads to higher crime rates, higher drug use, and higher dysfunction in family life among nonwhites. The American slaves were without education and property after emancipation, and it is not accidental—although it may not all be the result of specific individual intentions—that a large proportion of African Americans are still poor, undereducated, and without well-founded hope for socioeconomic advancement. Institutional racism continues through a kind of social inertia unless specific measures are taken to change it. When institutional racism is publicly recognized and whites do not want to change it, nonwhites may conclude that those whites who have advantageous positions in institutions within which nonwhites are less successful are classic racists.

Conditions of poverty create further aspects of institutional racism for nonwhites insofar as the poor, due to their lack of power and influence, may be victimized by the actions of more powerful groups. For example, places in poor urban and rural neighborhoods inhabited by nonwhites have in recent years been sites for toxic dumps and improperly processed garbage. Inadequate sewage removal, drinking water with high lead and bacteria counts, and vermin infestations are further examples of what has been called ***environmental racism*** in ghettos and barrios. Businesses that profit from the locations of such pollution defend their actions by claiming that they are not acting on the basis of race but in response to low property values. But whether some of the poor are more vulnerable to environmental depredation because they are poor, or because they are nonwhite, does not really matter in terms of the results. In addition to environmental and health damage, poor nonwhites become further ***stigmatized*** as people who live in filthy, unhealthful slums. Thus, vulnerabilities due to poverty that may itself be the historical effect of classic and institutional racism lead to further racism of both kinds.

The United States is a culture in which people gain social status and comfort in life by making money. The average middle-class American is impatient with and disapproving of those who fail economically over long periods of time. Because the belief in equal opportunity is strong, the poor tend to be blamed for their own plight. Those who are clients of human service and social welfare bureaucracies, all of which have had funding cuts in recent years, are begrudged this assistance by those who do not need it. When nonwhite race is added to such client status, further fuel is provided for classic racism. At this point classic racism intersects with another kind of "institutional" racism, this time the *institutionalization* of nonwhites.

C. NONWHITE RACISM

The educated liberal *consensus* seems to be that racism is something practiced by whites against nonwhites. But there are several objections to this liberal consensus. Black separatist rhetoric in the 1960s, as well as recent reactions to affirmative action programs that appear to privilege nonwhites over whites on the grounds of race, have led some people to insist that racism has no race. If some blacks, Indians, and Asians vilify whites, or say that all whites are cruel, not to be trusted, and generally evil, why isn't that racism? If black-owned businesses won't hire whites, isn't that a form of discrimination? Suppose a white person gets lost in a black neighborhood and is terrorized and beaten by blacks simply because he or she is white. Is that harm lessened by the fact that the victim's ancestors may have been oppressors? If nonwhites can be racists as well as whites, then why should white people bear all the moral and legal responsibility for being racists? Slavery and legal discrimination no longer exist, and even if blacks and other nonwhites are disproportionately poor, equal opportunity does exist for those who are exceptionally motivated. Therefore, why shouldn't nonwhites take the same responsibility for remedying their own racism that whites have been assigned for remedying theirs?

Answers to these questions depend on what is meant by racism. In the sense of classic racism, which entails individual motive and intent to harm those of a different race, nonwhites can be racists against whites. One objection to this claim has been that whites were the ones who invented the false concepts of race, especially the hierarchical concepts, and that whites are therefore the historically first and primary racists. However, while this objection may be persuasive as an historical or general cultural description, it does not lessen the possibility that a nonwhite person may be racist against whites in the sense of intending to harm them, either overtly or covertly, simply because they are white. That nonwhites have reasons justifying such harm makes no difference at all in their capacity to be classic (antiwhite) racists, because classic white racists also think they have reasons. Perhaps nonwhites, in having suffered more harm from whites than whites have suffered from them, have moral justification for their racism as a form of revenge. But conscious malice and hatred in the form of revenge are no less malice and hatred. Thus, classic racism would seem to be *"color-blind."*

However, institutional racism by nonwhites against whites is another matter. Since whites control most institutions and formal structures of power in the United States, nonwhites are not in a position to instigate, administer, and carry out institutionalized racism against whites. Apparent exceptions to institutionalized racism that privileges whites have been affirmative action policies for nonwhites, which will be discussed in Chapter 6. Insofar as most nonwhites who are presently concerned about racism are concerned about white institutional racism, they tend not to have a strong interest in seeking remedies for classic racism by nonwhites against whites. Morally wrong and personally disturbing though such racism is on an individual basis, it does not seem as important a social problem as white racism, either classic or institutional. Still, some critics have insisted that nonwhites behave unethically when they do not apply the same moral standards to their own behavior that are applied to the behavior of whites.

There is another form of nonwhite racism that deserves consideration here, namely nonwhite racism against other nonwhites. Some of it involves racism against members of one's own group, some against members of other nonwhite racial groups. In almost all cases, nonwhite-nonwhite racism often involves nonwhites taking up forms and expressions of white racism and directing them at nonwhites, either by harming them, hating them, or denying them opportunities. But nonwhite groups also sometimes develop distinct forms of nonwhite racism based on their own (nonwhite) perspectives. Nonwhite-nonwhite racism also involves issues of racial authenticity and loyalty that will be discussed under the subject of racial and ethnic identity in Chapter 8. Often, nonwhite-nonwhite racism is based on economic competition, for example, black-Hispanic tensions over jobs, and black condemnation of Asians who operate businesses in black communities.

Nonwhite-nonwhite racism also takes the form of colorism, or preference for light-skinned members within racial groups, and self-hatred of one's own nonwhite racial traits or aversion toward those in others. Many writers claim that all forms of nonwhite-nonwhite racism represent acceptance or internalization of white-nonwhite racism. However, whatever its causes, nonwhite-nonwhite racism may be more personally damaging than white-nonwhite racism. Most American nonwhites expect whites to be racist some of the time, but they also expect nonwhites in other groups to support them and nonwhites in their own group to accept them, or at least, not to display the kind of *aversive* behavior associated with classic white racism. Self-hatred on the grounds of race is an affliction that most people intuitively recognize to be self-defeating.

D. DISCUSSION QUESTIONS

1. In your view, do classic racists suffer from their racism? What do you think is the best remedy for classic racism?

2. Describe an act of covert racism and one of overt racism that you have directly experienced. (*Action* includes speech in this context.) Which do you think is morally worse, and why?

3. If someone accused you of being a racist, how would you try to prove them wrong?

4. Describe a contemporary institution or institutional practice that you believe is racist, or explain what is wrong with the concept of institutional racism.

5. Can nonwhites be racist against whites? Explain what you mean by *racist.*

E. RECOMMENDED READING

Opposing sides on punishing hate speech are Stanley Fish, "There's No Such Thing as Free Speech and It's a Good Thing," and Jonathan Rauch, "The Humanitarian Threat," both in Daniel Bonevac, ed., *Today's Moral Issues.*

For a primary source on white racism against blacks, see Andrew Macdonald, *The Turner Diaries.* A classic source on racism generally is Jean-Paul Sartre, *Anti-Semite and Jew.* For recent studies of racism see: Joel Kovel, *White Racism: A Psychohistory;* Stefan Kuhl, *The Nazi Connection: Eugenics, American Racism, and German National Socialism;* Michael Novick, *White Lies, White Power: The Fight Against White Supremacy and Reactionary Violence;* Patricia J. Williams, *The Rooster's Egg: On the Persistence of Prejudice.*

Contemporary philosophical analyses of racism include: Anthony Appiah, "Racisms," in David Theo Goldberg, ed., *Anatomy of Racism;* J. L. A. Garcia, "Racism as a Model for Understanding Sexism," in Naomi Zack, ed., *RACE/SEX;* Berel Lang, "Metaphysical Racism," and James P. Sterba, "Racism and Sexism: Their Common Ground," in *RACE/SEX;* Laurence Thomas, "Sexism and Racism: Some Conceptual Differences," in *Ethics;* Bernita C. Berry, "'I Just See People': Exercises in Learning the Effects of Racism and Sexism," and Marilyn Frye, "White Woman Feminist," both in Linda Bell and David Blumenfeld, eds., *Overcoming Sexism and Racism.* For a recent analysis of German anti-Semitism, see Berel Lang, *Act and Idea in the Nazi Genocide.*

On environmental racism, see: Cynthia Hamilton, "Women, Home and Community: The Struggle in an Urban Environment," in Alison Jagger, ed., *Living With Contradictions: Controversies in Feminist Social Ethics;* Laura Westra and Peter S. Wenz, eds., *Faces of Environmental Racism.*

Nonwhite-nonwhite aversion and racism is analyzed in general terms by Iris Marion Young in *Justice and the Politics of Difference,* chapter 5. In *The Bluest Eye,* Toni Morrison presents fictionalized case studies of black self-hatred and colorism. On this topic, see also Virginia R. Harris, "Prison of Color," in Jeanne Adleman and Gloria Enguídanos, eds., *Racism in the Lives of Women.*

Two of your male friends in high school grew up in single-parent households with incomes below the poverty line. Jeff is black and John is white. Both were B students and scored 1100 on their SATs. They applied to the same nearby college, intending to complete pre-law programs. Each requested full financial aid. Jeff was hoping for a scholarship based on Affirmative Action. John was hoping for a scholarship because his father had gone to the same college. Do you think that the three of you could have remained friends if only one of them got what he wanted?

CHAPTER 6

PUBLIC POLICY AND AFFIRMATIVE ACTION

INTRODUCTION

Public policy is the spirit and actions of the government and other public institutions regarding issues that affect citizens in important ways. Its literal foundation is a set of laws that have been crafted and passed by legislators who are presumed to represent the people. Its figurative foundation is the *intent of the law,* or what the goals of those laws are believed to be by government officials and the public. The reality of public policy in everyday life is determined by how laws are implemented by institutional and governmental administrators and interpreted by judges. When laws are just, public policy is the will of the people at their most informed, constructive, benevolent, and optimistic. When laws are unjust, public policy enforces ignorance, destruction, malevolence, and pessimism. During slavery, American public policy regarding race rendered blacks less than human in civic life because they had no rights or legal status as persons. During segregation, public policy regarding race was what today would be called racist. Current public policy for racial equality rests on three important pieces of federal legislation from the 1960s: the Civil Rights Act of 1964 prohibits discrimination on the grounds of race in all major American institutions; the Voting Rights Act of 1965 protects the voting rights of all Americans; the 1965 Immigration Act forbids exclusion based on race or national origin. However, while there is widespread formal commitment to racial egalitarianism, appropriate implementation of these laws remains a matter of controversy.

Resolution of the controversies about racially egalitarian public policy depends on what is meant by equality, how social inequality associated with racial difference is explained, and what people are willing to give up to achieve full racial equality. At this time, the *trope*—that is, the part that symbolizes the whole—of contemporary controversies about racially egalitarian public policy is ***affirmative action*** in the contexts of education and employment. Therefore this chapter is mostly about affirmative action in those contexts, although broader aspects of affirmative action are also considered, as well as other public policy issues involving race. At present, affirmative action remains in place in many American institutions and organizations. However, on some local levels, such as the California higher education system, affirmative action based on race has been eliminated due to popular demand. It is too soon to tell what the long-term effects of this change will be. This chapter focuses on the conceptual foundations for affirmative action and the assumptions behind criticism against it. Section A describes different types of affirmative action and presents arguments in favor of them. Section B presents arguments against affirmative action and considers several of the problems caused by it. Section C develops further discussion of the issues raised by affirmative action.

A. The Meaning and Assets of Affirmative Action

Affirmative action is a proactive attempt to correct inequalities due to race by *affirming,* or taking positive action for, those who are disadvantaged on the grounds of race. Affirmative action thereby involves assisting the disadvantaged, rather than prosecuting those who impose disadvantages on others. Attention to those who are in positions to discriminate on the basis of race, while it might also lead to racial equality, is not affirmative in this sense.

Critics of affirmative action often lose sight of the fact that it was originally designed as a strategic remedy for existing discrimination on the basis of race. An example of such discrimination is nonwhite applicants having equal or higher qualifications for admission or employment compared to white applicants, but not gaining entry. Before the 1960s civil rights legislation, disproportionately small numbers of nonwhites attended college and even fewer were managers or professionals. Discrimination on the basis of race could not be proved when policies of exclusion were implicit, either because no records were kept of qualified nonwhite applicants, or because admitting and hiring authorities sometimes claimed to reject nonwhite applicants for reasons unrelated to race.

The broad assumption behind affirmative action as a public policy strategy is that human abilities are equally distributed across races. If there are situations in which members of one racial group never get chosen when they apply for entry, or if significantly fewer members of that racial group, relative to their proportion of a larger population, get chosen than of another racial group, the conclusion based on this unequal *outcome* is that racial discrimination has been practiced. Explicit or overt racial discrimination is simple to prove because it proves itself: those who practice it say that is what they are doing. But implicit or covert racial discrimination is very difficult to prove in any one particular case because people who discriminate can conceal the real reasons and motives behind who they choose and who they reject. Therefore, given evidence of discrimination in the form of outcomes, the remedy is to legally require the hire or admission of individuals from the groups that are known to have suffered discrimination in the past and that are "underrepresented" in the present context.

Affirmative action has been implemented in a variety of ways where the groups affirmed have been white women, and black, Hispanic, and Indian men and women. Usually, if women are the affirmed group, white women tend to benefit. If nonwhite races are the affirmed groups, both nonwhite men and nonwhite women benefit. Some writers claim that when institutions are opposed to affirmative action they prefer to hire nonwhite women over nonwhite men because each hiree can be counted as a member of two underrepresented groups. But if institutions are sensitive to the high unemployment statistics for black men, they may prefer to hire them over black women who are equally qualified. Entrenched biases in favor of men generally may privilege nonwhite men over nonwhite women. Which group will be affirmed may also depend on the existing racial and gender balance in the particular context. For example, a company with all-male management, of all races, might focus on promoting women, whereas a coed college with very few students of color might focus on admitting more students of color, regardless of gender.

The type of affirmative action that is applied in specific contexts also varies. In some situations, it is decided that a specific number of women or nonwhites need to be included. This policy of aiming for *quotas* of women or nonwhites has drawn the heaviest opposition on the grounds that a predetermined quota of women or nonwhites means that a certain number of white men will not be hired or admitted, even if they are the most highly qualified applicants. As an alternative to quotas, in some situations special job lines or educational programs have been created for nonwhite applicants, in addition to the places that previously existed. This practice of adding places means that nonwhites are simply added to preexisting situations in which they previously were not present. The rationale is that the total number of opportunities are increased rather than redistributed.

Besides quotas and added places for nonwhites, affirmative action strategies may involve a reconsideration of criteria for entry. It may be decided that some of the criteria for entry privilege whites over nonwhites in ways that are not related to job or educational performance. For example, the high cost of private education may be more difficult for families of nonwhite students to afford; aptitude tests may presuppose that applicants have had cultural experiences that whites have had more often than nonwhites. Sometimes there is a deliberate policy of *preferential treatment* so that race is counted as a criterion for entry, with the result that successful nonwhite candidates may, apart from race, be equally or less qualified for the position than some unsuccessful white candidates.

Finally, there are business and institutional practices of recruiting applicant pools that are racially diverse. Such applicant pools may have a higher percentage of nonwhites than usually apply or than are present in the wider population. The most highly qualified applicants are then chosen, regardless of race. The rationale for these practices is that it gives nonwhites opportunities to be considered for positions for which they might not otherwise apply.

We will now consider four main arguments for affirmative action in the context of race. First, in situations where discrimination was practiced, qualified nonwhite candidates were often passed over solely because they were nonwhite. Such practices were unjust, and affirmative action in all of its forms works as a remedy for them.

The second, third, and fourth arguments are advanced in favor of affirmative action when whites would have otherwise been chosen, on their merits, in favor of nonwhites. Argument two is the ***role-model argument:*** Nonwhites in educational and professional positions where they were previously not present function as models for other, especially younger, members of their racial group who can identify with them and form realistic goals to occupy the same roles themselves. Eventually, this role-model emulation process will create social and economic equality across race.

Argument three for affirmation action is based on the concepts of ***compensation*** and ***reparation.*** Members of a society who are disadvantaged through no fault of their own, such as earthquake victims and people who have a history of discrimination and oppression based on race, ought to be compensated so that they have the same opportunity for success as members of society who are not thus disadvantaged. Quotas based on race, extra places and preferential treatment provide this kind of compensation to nonwhites. Reparation entails both compensation and the recognition of past injustice, in that benefits given now are intended to redress harms in the past. According to the reparation argument, affirmative action for nonwhites today is morally just not only because it creates equal opportunity for contemporary nonwhites but because it begins to make up for past injustice. While affirmative action in employment and education cannot repay the damage done to human lives during slavery and segregation, or even begin to make restitution for the value of the work done by slaves or the value of land taken from Indians, present affirmative action programs nevertheless are a step in the direction of this kind of redress.

The fourth argument for affirmative action is that it gives places and opportunities to particular nonwhite individuals who might not otherwise have them. The benefits to those people are concrete and direct and they enhance their chances for security, fulfillment, and happiness in life. If one can't change the whole of society, sometimes the best that can be done is to make life better for particular individuals, one at a time.

Finally, all forms of affirmative action focus on individuals and groups who have been otherwise passed over and rejected. Quotas, preferential treatment, role models, diverse applicant pools, and benefits to specific individuals all express welcome, approval, validation, and support. Such affirmation satisfies human needs for honor and esteem among those who have previously been deprived of that kind of positive attention.

B. THE DEBITS OF AFFIRMATIVE ACTION ▬▬▬

There are arguments against affirmative action from those who think it does not go far enough in correcting racial inequality, and those who think it goes too far. We'll start with the first group. It has been claimed that affirmative action does not really address discrimination. All who benefit from racial affirmative action have to be identified and selected on the grounds of nonwhite race. Since nonwhite race already bears a social stigma in American society, affirmative action candidates are marked as less desirable than whites, from the beginning. Many Americans believe that non-whites are less competent or less qualified than whites, and that this is why they need affirmative action in order to be admitted or hired. Therefore, the presence of non-whites in contexts where affirmative action is known to be in effect in itself will cloud future perceptions of their performance and recreate discrimination based on race within the newly integrated context. The result is that affirmative action does not remedy discrimination against nonwhites but may make it worse.

While affirmative action has been an effective form of compensation for those individuals who have secured educational and employment positions they would not have without it, it is not conclusive that their general opportunities in society are any better than they were before affirmative action. Where would those individuals be and how would they fare if affirmative action were suddenly curtailed as a public policy? If they would be no better off than they were before affirmative action was initiated, then affirmative action probably corrects symptoms of racism without addressing its causes.

As a form of reparation, affirmative action doesn't begin to make amends. A stigmatized place in an Ivy League college that a black student might otherwise be academically qualified for, is not adequate reparation for the rape of a slave great-grandmother or the lifelong labor of other enslaved forebears; neither does it repair the damage suffered during a childhood in a ghetto. A job on a construction site, as part of a quota, does not adequately repay a Native American for the loss of the un-spoiled natural environment that his ancestors got their living from on that same high-rise site.

Finally, it has been claimed that affirmative action has not gone far enough in correcting the situations of poverty and social dysfunction in American inner cities. Most affirmative action programs benefit the minority of nonwhites who are already part of the middle class. Affirmative action does not help the black underclass to gain entry into the middle class or even into the working class. There are no affirmative action policies in businesses that hire unskilled laborers because minority workers are typically already overrepresented on the lowest rungs in such firms; promotion to managerial positions in these firms is often not monitored in terms of race even though such firms embody the most extreme forms of institutionalized racism. Young people growing up in violent, impoverished, drug-trafficking neighborhoods have little reason to believe that they can ever emulate the few nonwhite role models in prestigious professional positions. The values held by nonwhites in those affirmative action positions do not speak to immediate underclass needs for survival; and the rewards for the hard work and self-discipline necessary to fit into the white mainstream cannot compete with the immediate gratifications of drugs and violence to which inner-city youth are continually exposed.

More radically, it has been claimed that affirmative action is no more than a pressure valve for those nonwhites who might otherwise direct their energies toward helping their entire disadvantaged groups. Indeed, the Kerner Commission's 1968 reports on riots in American inner cities may have provided the motive of social stability to some architects of subsequent affirmative action programs.

The most radical position against affirmative action on the grounds that it does not go far enough would be to interpret it as a white conspiracy to entice talented and enterprising nonwhites to "sell out." On this view, the beneficiaries of affirmative action exchange their real positions as members of oppressed and despised groups for the opportunity to reap material rewards as *tokens* of these groups in what remain white racist institutions. And after these beneficiaries of affirmative action leave their disadvantaged communities, they are no longer in positions to help those who remain in the underclass, and neither are they motivated to do so.

The arguments against affirmative action on the grounds that it goes too far are based on core American values of fairness and the belief in *meritocracy.* The unfairness of affirmative action is that race is taken into account in contexts where rewards should have nothing to do with race. If it is wrong to discriminate *against* people on the basis of race, then it is also wrong to discriminate *for* people on the basis of race. Since discrimination for nonwhites often requires discrimination against whites, affirmative action has been called *reverse discrimination.* Quotas and preferential treatment are examples of such reverse discrimination. Where special places are created for nonwhites, there is no unfair discrimination against whites. However, the special-place form of affirmative action is unfair in rewarding people on the basis of race, which ought not in itself to be grounds for reward, any more than it ought to be grounds for punishment. These extra places may be instances of "make-work" or create a tier of performance in which standards are lower, both of which waste resources.

For thousands of years, philosophers have defined *justice* as equal treatment for equal actions, virtues, vices, talents, and so on. In education and employment, what ought to count for advancement is ability and merit. Race is not a mark of ability or merit. Therefore, race ought not to count. This argument against affirmative action goes further. If ability and achievement are strong positive values, then affirmative action is a social evil because it fails to reward excellence for both whites and nonwhites. Nonwhites do not have to be excellent under affirmative action policies because they can succeed on the basis of race alone. Whites may not be rewarded for the attainment of excellence because less qualified nonwhites may be rewarded instead. If excellence is not rewarded, then individuals have no incentive to cultivate it. Part of the cultivation of excellence requires a willingness to seek out opportunities for advancement based on one's merits. And all forms of affirmative action discourage this kind of enterprise, including efforts to diversify "applicant pools." So the argument goes.

The arguments against affirmative action as forms of compensation and reparation rest on the claim that since discrimination and segregation on the grounds of race are now illegal, equal opportunity for nonwhites exists. If nonwhites remain underrepresented in mainstream American institutions and are disproportionately poor, it is their own responsibility and ought not to require sacrifice from members of other racial groups. Therefore, there is no need for compensation on the grounds of race and that justification for affirmative action collapses.

Reparation has been rejected by affirmative action critics because the white individuals alive today are not the individuals who committed the exploitative and oppressive acts against nonwhites in the past. Therefore, it is morally wrong to expect contemporary whites to give up benefits they deserve in order to redress the injustices of some of their ancestors. Human culture develops and progresses by putting the past behind it. If it were the responsibility of every generation to correct the wrongs of every past system of oppression that took place in history, then no one would be able to make their own plans and carry on with their own lives in the present. If it is argued that whites alive today still enjoy privileges that they have inherited as members of a group that has historically oppressed nonwhites, the question arises of where reparation is to begin. The crimes and exploitation against blacks took place on land that whites had stolen from Native Americans. Shouldn't we therefore return the land to the Indians as a first gesture of reparation? But even this would be inadequate because much of the land has been changed, so it would no longer be possible for Indians to live on it as their ancestors did. Since the past cannot be undone, we have to accept things as we've inherited them, behave fairly in the present, and move on in a system where people are rewarded based on their merit alone.

The role-model argument for affirmative action twists the meaning of *"role model."* Suppose a nonwhite is hired as a teacher through affirmative action. The role in question is the role of teacher. So why should the race of the teacher make a difference? If the role is the role of a nonwhite, the social value is dubious because it further divides people along the lines of race and distracts from job performance that has nothing to do with race. The proper roles of teachers, other professionals, students, and employees is to do the work their jobs require, not to "model" their jobs for other members of their races.

Concerning the benefits to specific individuals who are successful affirmative action candidates, while good is done in the short term, it is unearned gain. Such benefits from affirmative action are no different from winning a lottery or finding money in the street, and we have a right to expect something more dependent on skill than luck in filling places in education, the professions, and management.

C. FURTHER DISCUSSION

A big background difference between the ethical arguments for affirmative action and those against it is the time frame that is taken into account. Those in favor of affirmative action consider the history of nonwhites in American society and assume that present public policy ought to deliberately take that history into account. Those who are against affirmative action based on its unfairness to whites apply their ethical standards to immediate situations in the present. The question of the extent to which present generations are responsible for past history turns on the extent to which that history still has an effect. If one believes that the reason African Americans do not do as well, compared to whites, in education and employment is that they are still hampered by a history of exploitation and oppression, then that history is by no means behind us. Furthermore, if one believes that there is broad institutional racism in contemporary American society, then the objection to affirmative action that is based on present equal opportunity, collapses.

The disagreement about the appropriateness of reparation is another matter. While those white males who lose out to affirmative action candidates are not directly responsible for past racism, they are members of a group that has generally benefited at the expense of victims of past racism. In this sense, it could be argued that whites have a *collective responsibility* for past harms done to blacks, just as contemporary Germans have accepted a collective responsibility for harm done to Jews by the Nazis during World War II. Also, some defenders of affirmative action insist that reparation needs to be made for contemporary institutional racism.

While the appeals to merit are ethically sound, there is a real question of whether American society does generally dispense rewards on the basis of merit. Those (known as "legacees") who apply to colleges that their parents and grandparents attended are routinely given preferential treatment over other applicants. Fewer nonwhites than whites have parents and grandparents who went to college, because it is only recently, since the 1960s, that American colleges have not discriminated against nonwhites. Entry into, and subsequent success within, business and professional fields is to a large extent dependent on family and friend networking that traditionally has excluded nonwhites. If these two examples of preference for whites, which are built into the system, are examples of institutional affirmative action for whites, then why shouldn't there be a proactive public policy of affirmative action for nonwhites? To this, it might be countered that two wrongs do not make a right. But in that case, it would seem to be up to the critics of affirmative action to propose an alternative counterbalance to institutionalized white affirmative action.

The criticism of the role-model argument for affirmative action, like the argument from merit, fails to take existing social reality into account. In many fields, whites have dominated historically and there have been very few or no nonwhites. The new presence of nonwhites in such fields is very likely to send a motivational message to other nonwhites that race is not a barrier to entry. Such messages are important because many nonwhites assume that situations in which members of their race are not present are deliberately racist against them. Role models also work as points of identification. Young people, especially, look to older persons with whom they can identify as inspiration for their future goals. Such identification also furthers senses of belonging to successful groups. In a society as divided by race as ours is, many young people can only succeed in identifying with members of their same race. While the role-model argument in favor of affirmative action does depend on shifting the meaning of "role" from job role to racial role, racial role models may be more effective than job role models, given socially real racial divisions. That is, the socially real irrationalities of race form *psychologies of race* in individuals. Advocates of social change have to *work with* these psychologies of race, through an understanding of existing human motivation rather than abstract argument.

While scholars and social critics have been debating the merits of affirmative action, many American businesses have instituted affirmative action policies on their own, for several reasons. One reason is an obvious desire to avoid the appearance of discrimination and to decrease exposure to lawsuits based on discrimination. But another reason is that the placement of minorities in positions where they were not present before is good for business and for the image of business in the community. Affirmative action is recognized to be good for business because many American consumers are nonwhite and the American economy is two-thirds driven by consumer purchases. The image of business as socially responsive is not merely a pragmatic asset that enhances profit. Some members of the corporate community feel that due to the major effects of American business and its practices on American life, American corporations have a moral obligation to behave well, as social entities in their own right.

In conclusion, it should be noted that in all institutions where there are affirmative action programs, applicants, students, and/or personnel are automatically categorized by race. Except for people who **pass** for white, nonwhites have no choice about whether or not they will be the beneficiaries of affirmative action in such institutions. It is therefore beside the point to expect nonwhites to develop positions on affirmative action as though they were free to choose whether or not to participate in it.

D. DISCUSSION QUESTIONS

1. What in your view, is the strongest argument in favor of affirmative action for nonwhites?

2. What in your view, is the strongest argument against affirmative action for nonwhites?

3. Do you think that compensation and/or reparation are sound reasons for affirmative action?

4. Does affirmative action address racial discrimination?

5. Can you think of a remedy for racial discrimination other than affirmative action? Explain what its benefits might be.

E. RECOMMENDED READING

On the notions of affirming and affirmation, see Laurence Thomas, "Moral Flourishing in an Unjust World," in *Journal of Moral Education.*

For discussion of general social and political assumptions that underlie debates about affirmative action, see James P. Sterba, *Contemporary Social and Political Philosophy.* Further developments of these core political questions involving individual and group rights can be found in: William Alonso and Paul Starr, eds., *The Politics of Numbers;* Derrick Bell, *And We Are Not Saved: The Elusive Quest for Racial Justice;* Nathan Glazer, "Individual Rights Against Group Rights," in Will Kymlicka, ed., *The Rights of Minority Cultures.*

Sources that directly take up affirmative action include: Anita L. Allen, "The Role Model Argument and Faculty Diversity," in John P. Pittman, ed., *African-American Perspectives and Philosophical Traditions;* Bernard Boxill, "The Morality of Reparation," in *Social Theory and Practice;* Gertrude Ezorsky, *Racism and Justice;* Andrew Hacker, "Goodbye to Affirmative Action?" *New York Review of Books;* J. Edward Kellough, "Affirmative Action in Government Employment," *The Annals;* Lisa H. Newton, "Reverse Discrimination as Unjustified," in Allison Jagger, ed., *Liv-*

ing With Contradictions: Controversies in Feminist Social Ethics; Norma M. Riccucci, "Merit, Equity, and Test Validity," in *Administration and Society.*

On the pressure valve motive for affirmative action policy, see *The Kerner Report on Civil Disorders* and *The Kerner Report Revisited.* For discussion of socioeconomic problems that are untouched by affirmative action, see the following: Thomas Sowell, *Civil Rights: Rhetoric or Reality?;* William Julius Wilson, "Studying Inner-City Dislocations: The Challenge of Public Agenda Research," in *American Sociological Review;* and *The Truly Disadvantaged.*

CHAPTER 7

WHITENESS

INTRODUCTION

According to the *taxonomy* of race, over three-quarters of the world's population is nonwhite: Asian, Indian, black, and mixed. Even if one begins by viewing races as no more than biological types, it immediately becomes clear, on a global socioeconomic basis, that racial difference is not mere biological variety. Racial differences are accompanied by significant differences in wealth, military power, comfort in lifestyle, access to the most up-to-date consumer products, and technological expertise. While the racial taxonomy is superficial and even false in biological terms, it is a remarkably accurate device for picking out the socioeconomic differences. That this should be so is the result of historical events: the descendants of the groups of people whose members invented the racial taxonomy according to which they were white, are now the groups of people who have the most wealth, power, possessions, and technology. If we define the world by its dominant groups, the world is white. If we define a country by its dominant groups, the United States is white. Notice that in the case of the world, its whiteness is not a matter of numerical majority. What has been called the "browning of America," through white-nonwhite intermarriage and the increase in nonwhite populations due to recent Hispanic and Asian immigration, symbolizes both the numerical decrease of whites as a majority and progress toward equality among white and nonwhite groups.

The world was not always white and the United States did not automatically become white. American whiteness was constructed in several ways: through cultural ideals about whiteness, the development and enforcement of ideas of nonwhites as humanly inferior to whites, the exclusion of nonwhites from positions of public visibility, and the imposition of white cultural norms on all racial groups.

If one values the achievements of Western culture over the past three hundred years, and one accepts or makes a commitment to a mainstream American identity, the tragedy of whiteness is that blacks, Asians, and Indians have not been able to fully participate in it. That is, the tragedy of whiteness is that not everyone is white. If one thinks that Western culture, and particularly American culture, represent a long wrong path in human history because it has been taken at the expense of nonwhites, then the tragedy of whiteness is its very existence. That is, the tragedy of whiteness is that no one should ever have been white. Most people, of course, take a position somewhere between these extremes that everyone or no one ought to be white. In fact, the extremes distort the realities of how nonwhites have contributed to the wealth and culture of Western civilization generally, and the United States in particular. The often unrecognized contributions of labor from Asians and Africans, of land and resources from colonized people, and of art and other cultural products from all nonwhite groups entail that all so-called racial groups have been part of European and American history.

The purpose of this chapter is to focus on whiteness. Section A presents a brief intellectual history of racial ideas of whiteness. Section B is an analysis of the ways in which whiteness has acquired a moral force in American culture. Section C is a discussion of issues and identities that have arisen in reaction to recent criticism of whiteness.

A. THE HISTORY OF IDEAS OF WHITENESS

Before the 1970s, historians, sociologists, and cultural critics often did not take racial difference and racism into account in studying American society. More recently, scholars in the humanities and social sciences have addressed the cultural formations of white racial identity, as a distinct subject, under the framework of ***whiteness studies***. Some of the main themes of that multidisciplinary subject will be explored in this section.

The modern idea of the white race did not begin as a biological concept but rather as a religious identity for most Europeans and an intellectual identity for the English. A small European slave trade in Africans filtered through Mediterranean countries from the time of ancient Greece and Rome until the beginnings of the industrial revolution and the modern colonial period. Africans were not the only groups enslaved during this time period and the moral justification for enslavement, where justification went beyond simple rights of conquerors, was that those enslaved were heathens, or non-Christians. This justification was an effect of the importance of Christianity as a basis for identity in the European groups that later became known as white. After the Copernican revolution, during the formation of modern science as a systematic enterprise in the mid-1600s, the founders of The Royal Society of London for the Improvement of Natural Knowledge described the English as a race possessed of a special intellectual genius.

The English led the European slave trade by the end of the seventeenth century, and, at that time, ideas of biological whiteness were not yet developed. At the beginning of the English slave trade, Queen Elizabeth I had expressed concern whether African slaves had consented to their captivity. Some early English slave-traders had qualms about enslaving those who had the same "form" or human shape that they did. This indicates that whiteness was not at that time a designation referring to skin color, and that skin color did not yet symbolize white racial identity. Neither was whiteness fully based on Christianness because slaves and other non-Christians could be converted to Christianity. Although the equation of animality with non-Europeans began early in Western history, claims that Africans, Indians, and Asians lacked souls did not prevail in the Christian tradition.

The modern racial definition of whites as a superior human subspecies had three main sources: development of the science of biology as a system for classifying life forms; new biological and geographical interpretations of the Bible; and colonialist domination of non-Europeans by Europeans. In the heyday of nineteenth-century *biologism,* whiteness was never just a matter of physical traits but of cultural superiority as well. Scholars of the period were steeped in the tradition that held ancient Greece and Rome to be the source of Western European achievements in the arts, technology, government, and science. Both the Greeks and Romans had described themselves as naturally superior to other groups, but the Greeks recognized cultural debts to Hebrews, Phoenicians, and Egyptians, none of whom were of the same "race" as they. Inspired by the new (false) biological taxonomy, nineteenth-century European classicists redescribed ancient culture as the product of white Greeks only. On this interpretation, Greece, and through Greek influence, Rome, became the racially white source of racially white modern European culture.

In the United States, by the mid-1800s, the white race was constructed by scholars in the top colleges and universities as "The Great Race," the only race responsible for all of the magnificent achievements of human history and the only race fit to rule itself and all others. There was some empirical attempt to give these claims a biological basis through measurements of human cranial size, brain size, and limb proportions. However, the data collected on anatomical comparisons among whites, blacks, and Asians is now recognized to have been flawed from the outset: comparisons of brain size did not take body size into account; evidence contradicting the hypothesis that white men had the largest brains was discarded; and there was outright falsification as well as reports of measurements that had never been made.

During the late nineteenth and early twentieth centuries, whiteness, as opposed to blackness, immigrant Europeanness, and American Indianness, became the rallying point and foundation for American patriotism. Twentieth-century European immigrants passed from their nonwhite miniraces or subraces into the ruling white race as they became fully American. White identity as a political national identity was used to override regional differences that might have prevented national unity if people who were not conscious of themselves as white expressed primary loyalties to their immediate communities. At the same time, the one-drop rule became the effective social criterion for blackness, so that whiteness came to mean pure whiteness (see Chapter 1). The result of the combination of nationalism with biologism was that white purity became a moral, social, and civic virtue.

As the United States came to occupy the entire continent and built up the wealth that would make it a world power, the center stage of American public events was occupied by white leaders, white heroes, and white achievers. The history of the United States as taught to schoolchildren was a story of deeds accomplished by white people. The main characters were men because history was public and the proper sphere of women was private. The approved roles for white American women were restricted to domestic duties, the enforcement of sexual morality, the spiritual uplift of men, and, of course, ruling the world by rocking the cradle. Christianity endured as the spiritual dimension of whiteness, and God and Jesus were pictorially depicted and popularly imagined as white men.

By the time of World War II, whiteness had become fully attached to the masculine virtues of Americanness, which included enterprise, individualism, self-reliance, courage, and fairness. After the majority of Americans publicly aspired to and gave a semblance of living up to these ideals, the false biological racial aspects of whiteness no longer required as much emphasis as a foundation for white identity. Whiteness had become the American human norm: it seemed to white folk as though they were the only folk, because they were the decent, law-abiding, hard-working, church-going, money-making, family-raising people in the United States— the American people.

B. WHITE NORMATIVITY

The term *normativity* captures an attitude that things ought to be a certain way and that their being that way is normal, to be taken for granted. Three aspects of white normativity will concern us here: the normalness of whiteness to American whites; the goodness of whiteness to American whites; and the imposition of this normal and good whiteness on nonwhites and its use as a standard for evaluating them.

The normalness of whiteness results from the simple fact that in a culture that is still largely segregated by race, white people interact with other white people in all of the important private and public aspects of their lives. If your family members are all white, your friends are white, most of your classmates are white, the people you date are white, the person you will marry is likely to be white, the leaders of your society are white, your teachers are white, and the person hiring you for your first job is white, two things happen simultaneously. First, you are not aware of your whiteness and the whiteness of those around you during most of your daily activities. And second, whiteness is the accepted and expected racial condition for you, and nonwhiteness and nonwhite people seem to be unusual. The result of taking whiteness for granted and reacting to nonwhiteness as an exception is that in the minds of white people, *persons,* those beings who can take effective action and are worthy of respect, are white.

The general, often unspoken sense of the moral goodness of values held by white Americans has complex, changing sources. Whiteness was defined as moral superiority according to the nineteenth-century race theorists, and it continues to be assumed that there is a white hegemony over spirituality, rationality, intelligence, and technological inventiveness and competence. The color white also symbolizes virtue, as opposed to sin, in Christian theology. In the visual arts, including contemporary film, video, and print media, most of the people who are presented as examples or embodiments of human beauty are white (and Christian). But the most important foundation for white goodness in American culture probably concerns money.

Americans have always been materialistic and entrepreneurial. Slavery was above all an agrarian business form and the frontiers of the West were pushed back due to farming, mining, and other commercial interests. The discrimination against newly arrived immigrants has always coincided with their exploitation as sources of cheap labor. Some scholars believe that the American working class never united in a politically self-conscious way because nonblack groups who toiled without complaint, such as poor whites in the South and immigrants from Ireland in the early 1900s, were partly rewarded with the label of whiteness. And whiteness in turn allowed them to continue to work hard for further material rewards. Nonwhite groups beginning from poverty worked as hard as poor whites, and often under worse conditions, but without the reward of full entry into the economic system. Full entry into the economic system usually results in managerial and other forms of intellectual and social work. Some of this "white collar" occupation would be pursued for its own sake. However, in the coin of the American realm, the rewards that are most broadly recognized are always material things that can be bought: bigger houses, finer cars, up-to-date appliances, electronic gadgets, fashionable clothes, exotic vacations, tuition for children at private schools, and better care of the body through state-of-the-art medical treatment, diet, exercise, and cosmetics.

Even relatively *nonmaterialistic* lifestyles require money: artists, writers, and musicians need jobs or patrons in order to sustain their creative efforts; ministers, social workers, and teachers need institutions to subsidize their callings; intellectuals need money to buy books. Because money is a value, the asset of whiteness for obtaining money further reinforces the goodness of whiteness.

The imposition of white values on nonwhites has two dimensions. First, it expresses an inclusive aspect of Americanness. White Germans offer an interesting contrast. German Jews who spoke German and had been part of German civic life for generations were not considered Germans by the Nazis, and German Turks who have been in Germany for generations are not recognized as Germans by white Germans today. But the white American ruling classes, in what amounts to a separation of race from ethnicity, expect and demand that everyone living in the United States be an American. (Even members of groups that are considered foreign, such as Asian Americans, are expected to try to be Americans.)

The second dimension of the imposition of white values on nonwhites applies to the circumstances resulting from ongoing poverty and a history of oppression that have led to cultural characteristics that depart from white ethnic norms. The historical causes of the cultural differences are overlooked by white Americans and the departure itself is seen as morally bad and pathological. The kind of attention paid to black family life in the twentieth century by social scientists and public administrators is a compelling example of this normativity. During slavery, American blacks were not permitted to stay together as nuclear families. After slavery, in a culture where men were expected to financially support their families, black men did not have the same employment opportunities as white men. The result has been a black family structure that is different from the traditional white ideal. Black mothers have always had to work outside the home, black families are often extended in multigenerational and *collateral kinship* directions, and there are proportionally fewer black than white male heads of household. However, these adjustments to historical circumstances have been viewed by white observers as the willfully deviant cause, rather than the adaptive effect, of black people, especially black males, not succeeding in white American society.

C. POST-CRITICAL WHITE IDENTITIES

As nonwhites have affirmed and asserted their cultural differences from whites, many whites have come to believe that their whiteness is under attack. If whiteness is defined as a superior group and individual identity, and the values of white culture are believed to be proper values for all human beings regardless of their culture, then this belief is well grounded. But in an egalitarian society, there is no reason to regard any group as superior on the basis of false biological ideas of race or the results of unjust dominance. In a democratic pluralistic society, values arising out of distinct historical group circumstances become subject to public examination and debate if they are presented as values that everyone should hold. The values that are to be shared by all, except for foundational values of equal civil liberties and respect for human rights, become subject to negotiation. In these senses, it is unfair white privilege that is under attack and such privilege is difficult to defend except by physical force or rhetorical resistance to liberatory social change.

There are other ways in which whiteness is presently perceived to be under attack. If whites will no longer be a numerical majority due to white-nonwhite intermarriage (which results in more children being classified as nonwhite) and nonwhite immigration, then the result is less white people in the population. But it's not clear that this so-called "browning of America" is an attack on whiteness unless it is assumed that the main strength a group has is the size of its membership.

If nonwhites have the same *citizenship rights* as Americans that whites have, then an automatic association of whiteness with Americanness can no longer be justified. The same thing happens if nonwhites have the same *moral status* that whites have—it can no longer be assumed that whites are morally superior to nonwhites. Again, in an egalitarian society, this is not an attack on whiteness. But if the specific cultural practices and styles arising out of the ethnic groups to which whites belong, including WASP ethnicity that appears to be ethnically neutral, become devalued, driven underground, and suppressed, then whiteness is under attack. Such an attack against ways in which people live that do not harm others can be objected to by appeal to the same principles of justice that nonwhite groups use to protect their ethnicities.

Except for the last case, the foregoing perceived attacks on whiteness are not real harms because they do not deprive whites of basic rights or liberties. Rather, these affirmations of nonwhite cultural practices directly relate to improvements in the quality of the lives of American nonwhites. However, many whites have felt under attack on the grounds of their whiteness because they have been accused of being racist (see Chapter 5) and have been held *collectively responsible* for harms done to nonwhites by the ancestors of the groups to which they belong (see Chapter 6). There have been two lines of defense: The first has been to point out that not all whites, now or in the past, have lived the carefree lives of affluent oppressors or have held the values of the ruling class. For instance, some contemporary whites have ancestors who were peasants in Europe or who suffered religious persecution. The second line of defense concerns the present status of whites. Some whites who are not middle class have affirmed themselves as *white trash;* some whites who do not want to be identified as white, insofar as this means being oppressive against nonwhites, have identified themselves as *white race traitors.*

The label *white trash* used to be a form of abuse for poor whites who failed to conform to the moral standards and tastes of middle- and upper-class whites. Illegitimacy, alcoholism, drug addiction, incest, crime, illiteracy, domestic violence, irrationality, cheap personal possessions, substandard dwellings, sloppy housekeeping, dirty habits, undisciplined sexuality, and low I.Q.: these were the components of traditional stereotypes of white trash. The label and its stereotypes were ways of dismissing whites who failed to come up to middle-class white values and norms. Because they did not have the traits that were assumed by middle- and upper-class whites to distinguish whites from nonwhites, they were considered trash, beings of low value to be cast aside, discarded, not taken seriously.

Contemporary white trash affirmation is a sophisticated conceptual move against both well-off white discrimination against poor whites and nonwhite attacks on white identity. By affirming the tastes and lifestyles of poor whites, which are often determined by external economic conditions over which individuals have no direct control, a self-righteous and pompous aspect of white middle-class cultural mores is rejected. By affirming the whiteness of poor whites, white-trash advocates ask nonwhites to consider the fact that not all American whites belong to the social classes that are in positions of privilege and dominance over nonwhites. That is, some white people live in slums (both rural and urban), cannot afford adequate nutrition or health care, do not have home environments that can support their children's success in school, have friends and relatives in prison, and so on. White trash affirmation also constructs positive points of identity for some poor whites, as well as for some well-off whites who have "lowbrow" cultural tastes. However, white-trash affirmation retains an edge of racialist, if not racist, advantage. To be proud of being white trash is, at least in part, to be proud of being white. (Also, some members of the group referred to as white trash today were called "rednecks" not too long ago, and some rednecks have been known to be classic racists.)

White race traitors are contemporary writers and social critics who publicly accept responsibility for belonging to a group with a history of racism in both the classic and institutional senses (see Chapter 5). The acceptance of this responsibility is intended to relieve nonwhites of the burden of instructing whites on how not to be racist. The element of treason rests on a deliberate refusal to benefit from belonging to a group that sets the norms for all other groups. This is presented as a position of disloyalty toward other whites who accept the benefits. The term *traitor* also evokes the political nature of white racial identity insofar as the American ruling classes are white. Nonetheless, the polemical effectiveness of white race traitors depends on their retention of white racial identity at the same time that they disparage that identity and point out its injustices. If white-race traitors renounced their whiteness in action, by passing as nonwhites, they could not attack whiteness from within.

There are touches of playfulness in both white-trash affirmation and white-race treason. A more serious note is struck by contemporary white supremacists because they believe that racism against nonwhites has factual, aesthetic, and moral justification. Militant white supremacists advocate violent reaction against individuals who attack whiteness, as well as armed resistance, terrorism, and rebellion against federal and state government and other mainstream institutions that they think support non-whites against whites. Many white supremacists value what they believe is biological white racial purity. Some are ***fundamentalists*** concerning individual rights in their interpretations of the U.S. Constitution, and are committed to lifestyles that are independent of the contemporary American "system." A significant part of their ideology consists of the vilification of American blacks and Asians, and many believe in the existence of antiwhite and anti-Christian international Jewish conspiracies.

White supremacist groups partly overlap with libertarians, anarchists, Christian fundamentalists, and state and local constituted militia. Nonwhites, Jews, and mainstream political liberals and conservatives react to these types with varying degrees of fear, anger, and admiration. Contemporary ideologies of white supremacy are a nineteenth-century anachronism, and as such, they are ***radical*** (in the sense of returning to roots) reconstructions of whiteness under the stress of egalitarian gains made by nonwhites. The practical outcome of this extreme "neo-whitest" contribution to American history is presently undetermined.

D. DISCUSSION QUESTIONS

1. How do you think whiteness should be defined?

2. In your view, what moral justifications are there for the historical benefits that have accrued to white groups?

3. Describe some ways in which white culture has put itself on center stage.

4. Describe one or more white norms that you think ought not to be imposed on people with nonwhite cultural backgrounds, or on poor whites.

5. Do you think whites ought to "betray" their whiteness in the interests of social justice? What do you think would count as betrayal?

E. RECOMMENDED READING

On historical and global relationships between racial difference and money and power, see Thomas Sowell, *The Economics and Politics of Race: An International Perspective.*

David Stowe provides a useful survey of the relatively new field of whiteness studies in "*Un*Colored People: The Rise of Whiteness Studies," in *Lingua Franca.*

Scholarly analyses of the formation of the white racial category over modern history include: Virginia Domíguez, *White by Definition: Social Classification in Creole Louisiana;* Martin Bernal, *Black Athena: Vol I, The Fabrication of Ancient Greece, 1785–1985;* Reginald Horsman, *Race and Manifest Destiny;* Noel Ignatiev, *How the Irish Became White: Irish-Americans and African-Americans in 19th Century Philadelphia;* Michael Omi and Howard Winant, *Racial Formation in the U.S. 1960–1980;* David R. Roediger, *The Wages of Whiteness: Race and the Making of the American Working Class;* Naomi Zack, *Bachelors of Science: Seventeenth Century Identity, Then and Now,* chapter 12. On culture and class within white America, see

Lawrence W. Levine, *Highbrow/Lowbrow: The Emergence of Cultural Hierarchy in America.*

Recent works on contemporary whiteness include: Crispin Sartwell, *Act Like You Know: African-American Autobiography and White Identity;* Kate Davy, "Outing Whiteness: A Feminist/Lesbian Project," in *Theatre Journal;* Noel Ignatiev and John Garvey, eds., *Race Traitor;* Matt Wray and Annalee Newitz, eds., *White Trash: Race and Class;* Ruth Frankenberg, ed., *Displacing Whiteness: Essays in Social and Cultural Criticism.*

Popular works on white-trash affirmation include comedian Jeff Foxworthy's *Red Ain't Dead* and Dorothy Allison's novel, *Bastard Out of Carolina.*

James Ridgeway, in *Blood in the Face,* chronicles recent grassroots ideas of whiteness that many critics would consider racist.

I N THE PLACE WHERE YOU WORK OR GO TO SCHOOL, A GROUP OF YOUR OWN RACE OR ETHNICITY BANDS TOGETHER. YOU ARE ACCEPTED BY THEM BUT YOU ALSO ASSOCIATE WITH PEOPLE WHO DO NOT BAND TOGETHER ON THE BASIS OF RACE OR ETHNICITY. A MEMBER OF YOUR GROUP BECOMES THE SUBJECT OF A DISCIPLINARY INVESTIGATION. YOU DO NOT KNOW IF THIS PERSON IS INNOCENT OR GUILTY AND DECIDE TO KEEP AN OPEN MIND. BUT OTHER MEMBERS OF YOUR GROUP ARE EXPRESSING SUPPORT "NO MATTER WHAT." YOU EXPLAIN YOUR POSITION AND ARE TOLD IN RETURN THAT SOME MEMBERS OF YOUR GROUP HAVE ALWAYS WONDERED WHETHER YOU REALLY WERE ONE OF THEM. HOW DOES THIS ATTACK ON YOUR RACIAL OR ETHNIC IDENTITY MAKE YOU FEEL?

CHAPTER 8

RACIAL AND ETHNIC IDENTITY

INTRODUCTION

Racial and ethnic identity is perhaps the leading scholarly topic in current *emancipatory* studies. The term *identity* is ambiguous however, because it is used to mean both subjective experience and shared group membership that includes history and group self-image. For our purposes, a distinction between identity and *identification* will be useful: Identity is that about an individual that he or she reflects on, accepts, and develops, in the self. An individual has a range of choice about how to accept and develop his or her identity and it is unlikely to be based on any one thing. Profession, gender, family roles, race, ethnicity, and even sports, hobbies, and possessions might be part of identity. Identification is what others, typically those who do not know an individual well, use to distinguish that individual from others. Thus, black, white, Hispanic, Asian, woman, man, mother, teacher, lawyer, cop, are all terms of identification.

Despite this distinction between identity and identification, the sense of identity that is relevant to race and ethnicity is not entirely free of identification. To further specify how race and ethnicity relate to identity, racially and ethnically neutral meanings of identity are relevant. Psychologists and psychiatrists work with therapeutic notions of identity that refer to the feelings a person has about his or her self. For instance, someone confident and optimistic, who sets attainable goals, achieves them, and is not easily imposed upon by others, would be assessed as having a strong identity. Psychologically, a strong identity is connected with self-esteem and self-love that is based on trusting, nurturing interactions with caregivers early in life. Sociologists would be more likely to consider the identity of persons in terms of the roles they play in interacting with others in both personal and impersonal contexts. Theologians, by contrast, might locate personal identity in the soul or in the relation between the soul and God.

Philosophers have approached identity by asking what it is about a person that, if unchanged while all else about that person is changed, would lead observers to judge that the same person were still there. Sometimes it seems as though having the same memories is the criterion for someone being the same person. But lapses of memory or even amnesia do not change personal identity, from the perspective of others. Another philosophical position is that the sameness of a person is determined by a continuous path, through physical space, of the same human body, beginning at birth. Observers could, in principle, track that path of a person as a physical object and the continuity of the path would guarantee the sameness (identity) of the person. In addition to criteria for the sameness of persons, philosophers have addressed questions of what it is about persons that best characterizes them to themselves in an enduring way over time. Is it a mind, a body, a mind and a body, the ability to think, the ability to choose, memories? This philosophical concept of what one is to oneself, over time, is helpful to keep in mind in thinking about racial and ethnic identity. For example, if one could be the same person even though one's race changed, then racial identification would not be part of personal identity.

In Section A, the construction of nonwhite identities in *emancipatory traditions* is considered. The topic of identity is further explored through the idea of *authenticity* in Section B. The complexities of *American Jewish identity* in contemporary life are taken up in Section C, as a case study of ethnic identity.

A. NONWHITE EMANCIPATORY IDENTITIES ▪▪▪▪▪▪

Throughout American history, nonwhite emancipatory identities have been deliberately forged as resistance to and liberation from oppression. These emancipatory identities have included the moral virtues of courage against oppression, altruism toward other members of the group to be emancipated, and dedication to greater social justice in the future. Emancipatory identities cover the spectrum from fighting in political revolutions to religious uplift. Such identities are often based on a rewriting or retelling of historical events from the perspective of the oppressed group. We will consider such *socially constructed* aspects of emancipatory identities in this section.

When groups of people are oppressed, for instance, as slaves, low-paid laborers, or objects of racism, they are not automatically aware of their oppression as such. Those who are oppressed materially are often required to expend all their energy on the tasks of physical survival, getting the basics of food, clothing, housing, and safety in order to be able to carry on for another day or another week. Those who are psychologically degraded by racism may believe that they have the traits ascribed to them by dominant groups. At first, only a small number of the oppressed group, or members of another group who sympathize with their situation, find the words and do the deeds to create self-awareness of the conditions of oppression. Some form of group identity is necessary before an awareness of group oppression is possible. The most convenient and socially intelligible identity is often the identification made by oppressors: "n"egro, Negro, black, Jewish, Indian, "Oriental," Mexican, Hispanic, and so on.

The externally imposed group labels may be changed as the stereotypes associated with them by oppressors are repudiated by group members. For example, early twentieth-century African American leaders believed they had a mission to instruct their people, as well as whites, that they were entitled to education and the right to vote because they were not inferior to whites in the ways white society had constructed them to be. At that time they insisted that the small *n* in Negro be capitalized as the names of other American ethnic groups were. Similarly, Chinese- and Japanese-Americans now want to be known as Asians because the earlier designation "Oriental" was used to refer to imported objects as well as people, and its literal meaning was "East of Europe," suggesting that Europe was the center of the world. Indians have at different times preferred being called Native Americans in reference to their own origins, rather than the place (India) after which Europeans named them by mistake. Sometimes a new emancipatory group name is chosen in order to take on with pride what was intended to be a derogatory label, for example *black* or *queer.*

When labels are changed as parts of stereotypes are discarded, emancipatory identities are used to encourage and motivate actions that it is believed will result in social change. In a ***pluralistic society,*** they become the basis for what is known as ***identity politics.*** A general public policy commitment to pluralism presupposes that full social justice can best be obtained not if human rights are enforced on an individual basis, but if individuals receive protection and benefits as members of groups. This means that even though it is individuals who vote, the practical political unit is a group whose members share a common identity. Politicians running for office thus become concerned about securing the black vote, the Hispanic vote, the white working-class vote, the women's vote, and so on. Once elected, they are expected to support policies and legislation that will benefit the groups that helped put them in office. (Although their constituencies after election include those who voted against them as well—the President of the United States is president of all the people.)

Identity politics extends beyond politics in the narrow sense of electioneering. Contemporary debates over ***multiculturalism*** in education, the arts, and cultural life generally, are negotiations within identity politics. The rationale behind multiculturalism is that members of a pluralistic society who identify as members of minority groups ought to have an opportunity to see people like themselves in educational curricula and on the stage of public events. This speaks to a psychological need to be able to ***identify,*** that is, easily put oneself in the place of another. Multiculturalism also has a goal of universal intellectual and aesthetic enrichment through exposure to works and traditions that are different from those of the forebears of the racial or ethnic group to which one belongs. The centrality of white European cultural products and people, in a society where white Europeans are the dominant group, often makes it seem as though only these people and their products are of value and interest.

Even though emancipatory identities are deliberately constructed, this does not mean that they are experienced as superficial or artificial. Emancipatory identities are woven into racial or ethnic experience, such as traditions, shared circumstances of poverty over which members do not have the same control as more privileged groups, and most important, family life. It seems to be a universal fact for all societies in recorded history that human beings come into life in families, are raised in families, and look to family life for at least some of their deepest personal satisfactions as adults. Emancipatory identities are self-consciously taken up by families, even though the racial aspects of the identities were originally externally imposed by oppressive members of different groups. In the minds of individuals, the racial aspects of their identity become welded to the nurturing qualities of family life. Racially nonwhite and non-WASP Americans think of their families as black, Chinese, Mexican, Jewish, Irish, Italian, or mixed in ways that humanly redeem the malign origins of such categories as labels connoting inferior difference. Thus family life as well as public life can add a further dimension to the ways in which emancipatory identities counteract the alienation that accompanies membership in nondominant groups.

It should be recognized that not all aspects of racial and ethnic identity arise from situations of oppression or are deliberate reactions to oppression. Many people live in racially or ethnically *homogeneous* communities that have distinct practices passed on from generation to generation. These traditions, and the feelings of belonging and claiming that accompany them, are found rather than made or deliberately chosen by the individuals who grow up within them. And these individuals in turn pass them on to subsequent generations simply because it is the way they have been taught to conduct and celebrate their lives.

Reactive liberatory identities, family-based racial and ethnic identities, and positive identities based on community homogeneity all work together in dynamic processes that change as historical circumstances change. Each generation in a racial or ethnic tradition inherits the project of reinventing and discovering a shared group identity. A generation may break with its parents and relatives at the same time that it changes what it accepts from them in order to deal with changes in the wider society.

B. Authenticity

Indians, blacks, Asians, Jews, Chicano[/as], Latino[/as], and members of other groups that have experienced oppression in Western history are expected to be *authentic.* Racial and ethnic authenticity is usually presented as an obligation by those who are in a position to attach moral values to the racial and ethnic identity of the group in question. As a result, authenticity tends to be accepted as a duty by group members, especially younger people. The "authorities of authenticity" for any particular group vary from the immediate peers of teenagers to family elders, community leaders, and intellectuals. If the community is geographically scattered, its members are nonetheless expected to behave like group members through religious practice, marriage within the group, holiday celebration, dietary habits, and so forth. But perhaps more important than conformity to custom, an authentic group member is expected to help and support other members of the group simply because they are members of the group. An authentic group member is expected to feel fulfilled and gratified by his or her own authenticity, while someone who is inauthentic is expected to feel ashamed, inadequate, and morally weak.

However, the term *authenticity,* with its moral connotations, is ambiguous. People can be racially or ethnically authentic in one or more of at least five different ways. Let's suppose for the sake of this discussion that there is a racial or ethnic group—call it the Quicks—whose members have been stereotyped as follows: they are bald; they love to eat radishes; they traditionally collect insects; they listen to classical music at all major holidays and family gatherings; they are very generous; they are skillful liars.

One way of defining authenticity is as ***provenance.*** An authentic painting by Picasso has to be traced to the artist's studio through its successive owners, as well as certified to be a Picasso by examination of its brush strokes and its recognition as a Picasso by knowledgeable art dealers. A Quick with authentic provenance would be someone who had Quick ancestry and was known by members of his or her community to be a Quick. But suppose that this person—call her Winifred—did not like to be with other Quicks or to help them, claimed to hate radishes, preferred jazz to Bach, was seen wearing wigs, and known to be stingy. Peers and elders might then pronounce her inauthentic, despite her provenance, because she would not have an ***authentic appearance*** as a Quick.

Suppose that Winifred changed so that, in addition to her authentic provenance, she displayed the right kind of behavior, that is, she threw out the wigs, collected the insects, ate the radishes, rhapsodized over Bach, and lied elaborately, with the result that non-Quicks immediately recognized her as a Quick. If, in addition to this authentic Quick appearance, other Quicks knew they could count on Winifred's support and loyalty as a Quick, then Winifred would have ***authentic solidarity.***

Now let's imagine that economic conditions in the culture change, and Quicks, who previously lived in peace with other racial and ethnic groups, become a hated minority because they own (in perpetuity) exclusive patents to newly engineered genes for radishes that reverse aging and make people smarter. The majority group in society, the Dead, controls the mass media and thereby makes it common knowledge that the distinctive traits of Quicks are pathological signs of social dysfunction and moral degeneration. Over the next generation, during which Winifred's son Fred grows up, strong social pressures develop for Quicks to assimilate to mainstream Dead society, even though their civil liberties are legally protected and no one stops them from continuing in their traditional ways. Fred receives an elaborate glass ant farm on his sixteenth birthday and has a collection of 112 live crickets in gold filigree cages in his room. However, when his Dead friends come to hang out, he hides the insects in the garage. Fred loves radishes but when he is offered radish dishes at other people's houses, he pretends to be allergic to them. And, working against the stereotype of lying, Fred becomes known as a compulsive truth teller.

Winifred arrives at the painful realization that her son is inauthentic because he lacks the courage to express his real identity. She sadly reflects that even if truth telling were a virtue, Fred could not be considered virtuous because he tells the truth not because he thinks it's right, but because he doesn't want Dead people to dismiss him as a stereotypical Quick. If he just went ahead and allowed himself to *be* what he really was, he would have ***personal authenticity.*** But when Winifred tries to talk about this issue with Fred, his response is that it's very important to him to feel accepted by friends and know how to "move around" in the wider society. He also points out that many Quicks do the exact same things he does in order to "get along."

By contrast, Fred's sister Winnie hates radishes, is frightened of insects, likes rock 'n' roll, and refuses to lie because she believes that lying is wrong. Furthermore, Winnie insists that she has a right to be herself and that she will even marry a Dead man someday if she should happen to fall in love with one and he asks her to marry him. While Winifred disapproves of Winnie and recognizes that she lacks authentic solidarity as a Quick, she nonetheless concedes that Winnie, unlike Fred, is personally authentic. She hopes that this character trait will eventually result in Winnie becoming a more authentic Quick.

Referring back to the chapter introduction and Section A, we can draw the following conclusions about authenticity: authentic provenance is racial; authentic appearance is both racial and ethnic; authentic solidarity is political, in a broad sense; personal authenticity is a matter of strong psychological identity. Ideally, personal authenticity need not conflict with racial or ethnic authenticity. However, complexities of circumstance and individual personality make it difficult to generalize about the desirability of racial and ethnic authenticity. In fact, authenticity as it relates to membership in racial and ethnic groups varies as personal ***narratives*** or life stories vary. Because individuals are unique, they may be the best judges of what it means for them to be authentic members of their racial or ethnic groups. Thus, perhaps the forms of authenticity other than provenance ought to be subject to individual ***autonomy.*** In that case, the concept of authenticity, insofar as it means "genuineness" that is evident to others, loses much of its moral force.

From third-person perspectives, however, there is a stable meaning of authenticity that requires having knowledge of the history and values of one's group and displaying the knowledge and affirming the values. Such ***cultural authenticity*** may impose limits on individual autonomy, especially when individuals can benefit by downplaying the history of their racial or ethnic groups and affirming the values of the dominant group. Thus, cultural authenticity may be opposed to ***assimilation.*** If one thinks that individuals have a moral right to choose between cultural authenticity and assimilation, then the value of individual autonomy overrides the values of both cultural authenticity and assimilation.

C. CONTEMPORARY AMERICAN JEWISH IDENTITY

Contemporary American Jewish identity is a complex result of identity choices based on identity politics and all the different kinds of authenticity. Most other ethnic groups tend to place their religious, racial, or national origin labels before the word American. However, it seems to be customary to speak of American Jews, rather than Jewish Americans. American Indians are another exception to the general usage (although, when the label Native Americans is used, the second word does not mean the same thing as it does for non-Native Americans). The exceptions might be accidental or they might indicate that both Jewish and Indian identities are considered primary or prior to American nationality.

Since World War II, American Jews have largely been successful in projects requiring assimilation to mainstream American life. At the same time, many Jews still value their identities as Jews and struggle with questions about what it means, exactly, to *be* a Jew in the United States during the 1990s. Although Jews today generally define themselves as a religious group, there is religious difference among Orthodox, Reform, and Conservative Jews. Criteria for who is a Jew extend beyond religion to ancestry: According to Talmudic Law and Israel's immigration policy, which in principle keeps an open door to all Jews, a Jew is someone whose mother is or was a Jew or someone who has converted to Judaism according to Orthodox criteria. However, some insist that anyone whose father is a Jew, and who practices the religion but does not have a Jewish mother, is also a Jew. The religious aspect of Jewish identification entails that people whose mothers were not Jewish can convert to Judaism and thereby become Jews. The maternal heredity aspect of Judaism entails that people whose mothers are Jewish are Jews even if they are ***nonobservant,*** that is, do not practice the Jewish religion. Furthermore, some Jews see no contradiction in claiming both an ***atheistic*** belief structure and Jewish identity, with varying degrees of observance.

The formation of the state of Israel in 1948 allowed Jews worldwide to claim a homeland. Israel is accepted as the original homeland of Jews since biblical times. But throughout Western history, Jews dispersed to almost every country on earth, mainly as a result of their periodic persecution and expulsion from Christian countries, as well as Palestine, during crises of anti-Semitism. Some Jews who were not born in Israel and have no known ancestors born in Israel wonder how it is possible to have a homeland from which none of their known family members originated.

Zionism, as opposed to the different forms of Jewish religion, is partly a political ideology that privileges Israel as the center of Jewish life for all Jews. Since Israel is a small country whose neighbors resist its existence as a state, Israel has been involved in political and military actions that many Jews do not support on other political grounds. Some Jews insist that political support of Israel is now necessary for Jewish authenticity. Other Jews believe that their Jewish identity is independent of politics.

The success of Jews in mainstream American life has been accompanied by the abandonment of traditional cultural practices that derived from the lives of Jews in the specific European countries from which many emigrated in the late nineteenth and early twentieth century. Early twentieth-century Jewish immigrants in New York City had their own press and theatre in ***Yiddish,*** a dialect of High German that is written in Hebrew letters. Today, few American Jews speak, much less read Yiddish, although some adults can remember their grandparents' use of it. The official language of Israel is modern Hebrew and only a minority of American Jews are fluent in that.

Given that religion, ancestry, homeland, customs, and language are such variable components of Jewish identity, the question of Jewish identity is extremely problematic. At least 25 percent of all Jews who marry, marry non-Jews. Jewish identity is not imposed on American Jews in the same way that black identity is imposed on any

American with black ancestry, so this rate of intermarriage represents further loss of Jewish identity in family life.

For many Jews, thinking about the Nazi attempt at genocide intensifies Jewish identity; even casual, so-called "polite" American anti-Semitism that imputes stereotypes of appearance and behavior to Jews, can be a reason to retain Jewish identity. The psychological dynamic of Jewish identity is often reported as a process of discovery based on strong emotional reactions of horror, shock, fear, and grief in response to finding out about Jewish suffering. However, some Jews question the validity of an identity based on suffering. Others insist that the persistence of Jews, as Jews, in the face of such suffering is inspiring in universal human terms, so that remembering that they are Jews makes them better people.

Finally, race intersects with Jewishness in complicated ways: Although most Jews and non-Jewish white Americans consider Jews to be white, some black Americans and some Jews believe that Jews are nonwhite because they are traditionally *Semites.* Most American Jews are of European origin but a small number have black ancestry. Jews with black ancestry who live in Jewish communities tend to identify as Jews first and African Americans second. Jews with black ancestry who have been raised in, or as adults live in African American communities, tend to identify primarily as black. But blacks who have become Jewish through conversion tend to proclaim encompassing identities, that is, black and Jewish. The operative word in all this is *tend,* there are many exceptions to such generalizations.

D. DISCUSSION QUESTIONS

1. Name at least one leader of an emancipatory tradition and show how that person exemplifies the description of emancipatory identity in Section A, or fails to do so.

2. How would you defend multicultural innovation in an educational curriculum for high school students to someone who opposed it on the grounds that it would detract from teaching the classics of Western civilization? Or, if you wouldn't defend such innovation, why not?

3. What could be lost in a fulfilling life if one constructed an identity for oneself mainly based on authentic membership in a racial or ethnic minority group? What would be gained?

4. How would you explain Jewish identity to an intelligent child?

5. What are the components of your own identity?

E. RECOMMENDED READING

For philosophical analyses of personal identity, see: Harold W. Noonan, *Personal Identity,* and Naomi Zack, *Bachelors of Science: Seventeenth Century Identity, Then and Now,* introduction, chapters 4, 5, 6. For psychological discussion of identity, see: Erik Erikson, *Identity and the Life Cycle;* P. Hines and L. Berg-Cross, "Racial Differences in Global Self-Esteem," in *Journal of Social Psychology.* For philosophical and psychological issues relating to racial identity, see: Anthony Appiah's *In My Father's House,* and "'But Would That Still Be Me?'" in Naomi Zack, ed., *RACE/SEX;* Helena Jia Hershel, "Therapeutic Perspectives on Biracial Formation and Internalized Oppression," in Zack, ed., *American Mixed Race;* Howard McGary, "Alienation and the African-American Experience," in John P. Pittman, ed., *African-American Perspectives and Philosophical Traditions.*

For an overview of the issues involved in identity politics, see Iris Young, *Justice and the Politics of Difference,* chapter 6. For a theoretical discussion of multiculturalism, see David Theo Goldberg, ed., *Multiculturalism: A Critical Reader.*

On black authenticity, see Ralph Ellison's *Invisible Man.* For more political notions of black authenticity, see: Richard Wright, *Black Power: A Record of Reactions in a Land of Pathos,* and Wright's *The Outsider; The Autobiography of Malcolm X,* as told to Alex Haley; C. V. Willie, *Oreo: Race and Marginal Men and Women.* On black identity and social and philosophical issues, see Lucius T. Outlaw, *On Race and Philosophy.* See also Leonard Harris, ed. *Philosophy Born of Struggle: Anthology of Afro-American Philosophy from 1917.*

For a comparison of black and Jewish identity, see Laurence Mordekhai Thomas, *Vessels of Evil.* On problems with Jewish identity, see Laurie Shrage, "Ethnic Transgressions: Confessions of an Assimilated Jew," in Naomi Zack, ed., *American Mixed Race.* On mixed black and Jewish identity, see James McBride, *The Color of Water: A Black Man's Tribute to His White Mother,* and Naomi Zack, "On Being and Not-Being Black and Jewish," in Maria P. P. Root, ed., *The Multiracial Experience.* See also, David Theo Goldberg and Michael Krausz, eds., *Jewish Identity.*

The importance of skin color in black identity is examined in: Kathy Russell, Midge Wilson, and Ronald Hall, *The Color Complex: The Politics of Skin Color Among African Americans;* Judy Scales-Trent, *Notes of a White Black Woman;* Caroline A. Streeter, "Ambiguous Bodies: Locating Black/White Women in Cultural Representations," in Root, ed., *The Multiracial Experience;* Brunetta Wolfman, "Color Fades Over Time," in Naomi Zack, ed., *American Mixed Race.*

On Hispanic and Latin American identity, see: Gloria Anzuldúa, *Borderlands/La Frontera: The New Mestiza,* and Anzuldúa, ed., *Making Face, Making Soul;* Ofelia Schutte, *Cultural Identity and Social Liberation in Latin American Thought;* Richard Rodriguez, *Hunger of Memory: The Education of Richard Rodriguez.*

On Native American identity, see Alexandra Harmon, "When an Indian is Not an Indian? 'Friends of the Indian' and the Problem of Indian Identity," in *Journal of Ethnic Studies,* and M. Annette Jaimes, "Some Kind of Indian," in Zack, ed., *American Mixed Race.* For biographical sources, see Arnold Krupat, *Native American Autobiography: An Anthology.*

On Asian American identity, see Maxine Hong Kingston's *The Woman Warrior* for issues of Chinese-American identity. See also, Connie Kang, *Home was the Land of Morning Calm: A Saga of A Korean American Family.*

SOME WHITE MALE TEENAGERS IMITATE THE HAIRSTYLE, SPEECH, DRESS, AND BODY LANGUAGE OF BLACK MALE TEENAGERS. SOME BLACK FEMALE TEENAGERS IMITATE THE HAIRSTYLE, SPEECH, DRESS, AND BODY LANGUAGE OF WHITE FEMALE TEENAGERS. IT'S LESS COMMON FOR BLACK MALE TEENAGERS TO IMITATE THE STYLE OF WHITE MALE TEENAGERS OR FOR WHITE FEMALE TEENAGERS TO IMITATE THE STYLE OF BLACK FEMALE TEENAGERS. HOW WOULD YOU ACCOUNT FOR THESE DIFFERENCES?

CHAPTER 9

RACE AND GENDER

INTRODUCTION

In ordinary language, when people refer to sexual difference, they often do not distinguish between biological differences and social roles. However, many academic writers today attempt to draw this line with the distinction between *sex* and *gender:* The term *sex* refers to the inherited biological characteristics of being male or female. The term *gender* refers to the temperament and behavior within each sex, which includes sexual preferences, sexual roles, family roles, and broader roles in society, as well as aptitudes and mental and emotional dispositions. There is considerable difference of opinion about whether sex determines gender, or gender is learned and capable of being changed.

Differences in biological sex have an empirical foundation on a chromosomal level, and except for a small number of individuals, human beings appear to be *sexually dimorphic,* that is, sortable into male or female categories, exclusively. However, some feminist critics insist that sexual dimorphism simplifies a more complicated biological reality. Some infants are born *intersexed:* they may have the internal genitalia of one sex and the external genitalia of the other; their genitalia may be of a different sex than their chromosomes; or they may lack pronounced characteristics of either sex. When physicians resolve these situations by suppressing some sexual characteristics and enhancing others, a sexually *ambiguous* or *androgynous* reality is suppressed. This reality, because it emerges without human intervention, is in fact "natural."

While biological sex appears to be more fundamental than gender, other critics insist that this is true only of Western European cultures and only since the eighteenth century. In some non-Western cultural contexts, for example, *berdache* among Indians, male-bodied individuals who assume the social roles of women are accepted as women. Another example of how gender might be more fundamental than sex is evident in reports of ***transsexuals*** who claim to have known from an early age that despite the sex assigned to them (in our culture) based on their biology, they are in fact the "opposite" sex, or neither male nor female. If we accept that the introspections and longings of those whose gender is at odds with their assigned sex are not pathological, then biological sex is not always foundational for sexual identity.

Before the seventeenth century in Europe, gender was more stable than biological sex as a source of identity. For example, respected medical authorities believed that women who exercised too strenuously would raise their body temperature, which was normally lower than that of men. As a result, female genitalia, which were believed to be inverted male genitalia, could "pop out" and such women would become men—a phenomenon that several learned doctors claimed to have directly observed. During the sixteenth and seventeenth centuries, women who assumed male social roles, for example, Queen Elizabeth I, and the poet Aphra Behn, asserted that they had "masculine parts" which made such roles possible for them. (Queen Elizabeth insisted that she had the "heart and stomach of a king.")

From the early eighteenth century on in Western culture, male and female sexual difference has been closely associated with male and female gender difference. It has generally been assumed that men have the dominant social roles they do at least partly because of their biological sexual traits. For instance, male hormones are supposed to result in more aggressive behavior than female hormones. But men differ in their gender styles and in their degrees of masculinity, and women differ in their gender styles and degrees of femininity. The ways in which male or female gender are expressed are also influenced by social class.

People differ in sexual preferences for partners of opposite sex, same sex, or both opposite and same sex. To complicate matters even more, the gender of the sexual roles people enact may be different from their genders in nonsexual areas. For example, although aggression is associated with male gender and nonassertiveness with female gender, some heterosexual men are sexually nonassertive, while some heterosexual women are sexually aggressive.

Among all their variations, sex, gender, and sexuality are fundamental bases of identity and identification. In American life, race is also a very important, if not fundamental, basis of identity and identification; ethnicity often is as well. The two double categories of race/ethnicity and sex/gender intersect in ways that result in differences in gender among people of the same sex with different racial and ethnic identities. The intersection of race and sexuality is the topic of Chapter 10. In this chapter, we will focus on aspects of the ***intersection*** of gender and race. Black and white male gender is discussed in Section A, and black and white female gender in Section B. Section C is an introduction to some of the issues feminists have raised about race.

A. BLACK AND WHITE MALE GENDER

In American history, black male gender has always been disadvantaged in comparison with white. During slavery, black men had none of the civil rights white men did, and from the end of slavery until the 1960s, they were denied access to the education, employment, and civic status available to white men. Insofar as adult male gender is the result of achievement in education and work that is recognized through civic status, black American men have been deprived of the opportunities to construct male gender that have continually been available to white American men. In a society where men have traditionally been the main economic providers for their nuclear families, black men have been unable to fulfill that role due to institutionalized racism that restricted their earning power. Black men have therefore been unable to participate fully in the ***patriarchal system,*** in which men have been dominant over women personally, economically, professionally, intellectually, and politically.

The social and family roles associated with patriarchy gave white men control over the lives of their wives, daughters, and sisters, as well as the authority to protect them. Such roles were not available to black men in relation to black women during slavery, and after slavery, they were difficult for black men to construct. As a result, white slave-owners and, after slavery, white men generally were able to directly exert control over the lives of black women.

The widespread exclusion of black men from patriarchy has not prevented black men from aspiring to the power and authority more easily attainable by white men, nor has it prevented some black men from obtaining them. However, the exclusions and restrictions have made it more difficult for black men than white men to be patriarchal. Black men thus face issues of liberation in gender as well as race.

Along with the oppressive conditions of black male gender, black men have been stereotyped as lazy, irresponsible, lawless, lewd, and unintelligent. They are also assigned stereotypical occupational roles that many find oppressive or personally limiting: menial worker, criminal, preacher, substance abuser, Uncle Tom, athlete, entertainer, violent black man, etc. Missing from the range of normally attainable options are roles such as: doctor, college professor, scientist, chief executive of a large institution, self-made millionaire, well-to-do family man. Black men who attain and excel at nonstereotypical roles tend to be categorized as exceptional black men. The implication of the adjective "exceptional" in this case is that, because the kind of achievements taken for granted by white men are not accessible to most black men, when black men do attain them, they are odd and unusual. That is, the barriers to black male success are made to seem to be traits of individuals rather than social restrictions.

The stereotypical gender roles assigned to black men tend to become self-fulfilling prophecies for two reasons. First, it is human nature to aspire to what others define as normal and customary, especially when stepping outside those norms may result in punishment from members of more powerful groups in society. Second, in Western culture, manhood is something to be achieved by young men, rather than an automatic conclusion to boyhood. Adult male personal identity and self-esteem depend on having done what is necessary to become a man. The behavior and accomplishments that certify manhood are observed by a young man's male peers and elders who already know him. Male roles that fall outside or beyond the range anointed by peers and elders may be useless for attaining and proving manhood in a young man's social context. If these peers and elders base their own manhood on racial stereotypes, then the stereotypical roles become the most viable options through which manhood can be achieved.

The ways in which men are recognized and publicly honored for high achievement by other men and women and children form a second important dimension of masculinity in American culture. White men are recognized by people of both sexes, all ages, and all races as eligible for public honor in a society in which men are publicly honored more than women. Black men are not equally eligible for public honor. Government officials and the public take a much longer time to honor black men of high achievement for the same deeds that immediately bestow honor on white men. For example, American black men have fought in every war since the Revolutionary War but their contributions as soldiers have still not been fully acclaimed. At this writing (January 1997), black soldiers who deserved the Medal of Honor for bravery during World War II are being recognized for the first time, over fifty years later.

Blacks achieved full civil rights at about the same time the present wave of feminism began in the 1960s. Women are now able to support themselves financially and to defer or reject traditional roles of dependence on men. Many women now occupy prestigious occupational roles previously reserved for white men, and receive traditional male honors as well: there is a woman on the Supreme Court; women hold the posts of U.S. Attorney General and Secretary of State; women have been in military combat (a popular recent movie, *Courage Under Fire,* depicted a black officer [Denzel Washington] who vindicated the courage of a white female officer [Meg Ryan] during the Persian Gulf War); and there are now women college presidents, professors, lawyers, doctors, and scientists. In a complementary fashion, many men now participate fully in the nurturing aspects of family life, and most men today realize that it is important for them to be aware of their own and others' emotions, a kind of sensitivity traditionally restricted to women. Generally speaking, the increase in female participation in workplaces has been accompanied by scholarly and popular criticism of patriarchy, or traditional white male gender dominance.

Even though black men continue to be underrepresented in the gender roles retained by white men, they are also subject to criticism for some of the ways in which some of them have expressed their masculinity: harsh treatment of black women, sexual aggression toward all women, irresponsibility as fathers, criminal violence. Feminists criticize black male gender as part of patriarchy in the general sense, and white conservatives typically view black male gender as dangerously deviant. Thus black male gender is doubly disadvantaged: it lacks the social power of white male gender, and it is perceived to be an undesirably exaggerated variation on those aspects of male gender presumed to be based on masculine sexuality.

B. BLACK AND WHITE FEMALE GENDER

Before the 1970s, most middle- and upper-class American white women did not have economic or productive responsibilities outside the homes of their nuclear families. They were subordinate to men in the family and protected by men in situations outside the home. In contrast, since the Civil War black women have been caregivers in extended families and have worked outside their homes, as laborers and servants for whites, to support themselves and family members on the most basic levels of food, clothing, and housing. In the absence of black male patriarchs, they have often been heads of households and single parents, long before the problems of single parents began to receive serious attention and their status was deemed worthy of respect (to the extent that it now is). Black women have not been afforded the same physical and sexual protection that white men have given white women, and throughout most of American history, black men have been unable to protect them. The result of these historical differences in circumstance is a less "feminine" and more self-reliant form of gender for black women than white.

Some of the feminine roles denied black women have been rejected by many white women in recent decades. Nonetheless, the ways in which female gender is less feminine for black women have not amounted to a more liberated situation. This is clear in the ways black women are perceived, by men and women of both races, to fall short of ideals of female beauty and gender attractiveness.

American white normativity (see Chapter 6, Section B) has extended Western European ideals of female attractiveness and moral goodness to women of all races. These ideals derive from middle-class capitalist patterns of production that restricted women to the household. Before the 1600s, the majority of European households were extended social units of family members, servants, kin, and friends that produced their own wealth, necessities for survival and amenities by craft or agriculture. Everyone worked cooperatively within such households. After the 1600s, men worked in public places outside the home. European middle-class women were expected to take care of their households and families, and support the employment, civic, and social activities of their husbands. If their husbands and fathers had enough money, drudgery could be assigned to women less well sponsored and minor skills in the arts and music could be cultivated.

The female ideal, set by affluent families, was a physically weak but graceful creature, pleasant, tactful, intellectually superficial, and refined in manners and taste. Her sexuality was muted and she was expected to be spiritually uplifting to men. She was desired to have pale skin, flowing fine-textured hair, and delicate facial features. Her hairstyle, clothes, and other personal accessories were designed to emphasize her "natural" endowments. These ideals of white female virtue and beauty have been unattainable by American black women, as much due to economic and social circumstances as to differences in skin color, hair texture, and facial morphology. It is easy to imagine that if black women or Asian women had been the members of the dominant leisure class, beauty ideals would have been based on their hereditary physical traits. The fact that rich white men were willing to subsidize white women of their class as decorative objects, is probably the main reason for beauty ideals having been centered on white physical types. Most poor white women who could not become "ladies" in this way were aesthetically devalued. This exclusion of poor white women from the category of most desired white women further emphasizes the importance of social class in creating ideals of female beauty.

The aesthetic result of white dominance has been a devaluation of black female attractiveness and beauty, by both whites and blacks. Black women who are held up as models of female beauty still tend to resemble white European ideals, often because they are mixed race. This further burdens black women who do not resemble white ideals of beauty. In black culture, as well as white, beauty is an important part of female self-esteem. If some black women are precluded from being beautiful within their own culture, as well as white culture, then their self-esteem as women is potentially diminished. Of course, in any culture, not all women are considered beautiful. But it is particularly cruel when some women are denied consideration solely on what are perceived to be racial grounds when these grounds have nothing to do with the other standards of beauty, such as health, grace, symmetry, and so forth.

The liabilities of the intersection of female sex and black race for black women (which creates a distinct gender) are also evident in the kinds of occupational roles to which they have been restricted. They have been stereotyped as nurturing, scheming, lewd, and unintelligent. Like black men, they are typically assigned personally limiting occupational roles: servant, laborer, mammy, prostitute, church lady, matriarch. While these roles often require near-heroic virtues of endurance, optimism, self-reliance, and altruism, they are all service roles. Black women who become professionals, entrepreneurs, or even successful entertainers are often viewed as "strong" black women or else perceived to be emotionally cold, selfish, and aggressive in unwomanly ways. What's missing from the traditional occupational roles for black women, to this day, is a wide-scale recognition of their intellectual competence. There are a few acclaimed black female novelists but very few black female public intellectuals; black female nurses but fewer doctors; primary school teachers but fewer high school and college teachers; meter maids, postal employees, and police but not as many lawyers, prosecutors, and judges proportionately. (The film and television media ambiguously play on this last situation with a propensity to cast black female actresses as judges. It's not clear whether this is meant to surprise everyone or encourage black women; whether it does encourage young black women to study for careers in law or intensifies white backlash against affirmative action, while at the same time mocking black female achievement.)

C. WOMEN OF COLOR AND FEMINISM

During the past two decades, Indian, Asian, Chicana, Latina, African American, and multi- and biracial women activists and scholars have constructed theories and descriptions of the lives of women of color in the United States. Some of their work has been developed as a criticism of earlier writing by white middle-class women in feminism and women's studies. Other strains of nonwhite feminism and women's studies have focused directly on goals and strategies for empowering American women of color.

The chief complaint from feminist women of color about white feminism is that white feminists have been preoccupied with themselves and their own middle-class problems in their liberatory efforts. The criticism charges white feminists with constructing a false essentialism of female gender that they have mistakenly assumed holds for all women, regardless of race, ethnicity, or social class. Many white feminist theorists have accepted this criticism and are presently struggling with questions of whether a unified, universal type of feminism is possible. They ask themselves what they can do to express solidarity with feminists of color. Still, racial divisions among feminists remain, partly due to the perceived need of feminist women of color that liberation on the grounds of race or ethnicity take place before liberation on the grounds of female gender in itself. Since white feminists are already liberated on the grounds of race, their ability to go directly to problems of gender is seen as a privilege that accrues to them by virtue of being white in a white racist society.

The problem of whether liberation on the grounds of race ought to take precedence over liberation on the grounds of gender has a long history in American political activism. Before the Civil War, there were strong alliances between those in favor of women's rights and abolitionists. Abolitionists, of course, wanted to end slavery and nineteenth-century feminists were concerned to secure both voting and property rights for women. After the Civil War, many of the former male abolitionists broke with the cause of women's rights and secured voting rights for black men. This infuriated the *suffragettes,* some of whom ignominiously tried to block passage of the Sixteenth Amendment. During Reconstruction, and throughout the years of segregation, women's rights groups excluded black women. Black women formed their own network of clubs, charities, and educational organizations that provided financial assistance and cultural encouragement within black communities.

After American women secured the vote in 1920, it became respectable for young middle-class white women to work before getting married, although career women were expected to remain single. During World War II, many American women participated in the defense industry and in support divisions of the military. After World War II, an economic boom was accompanied by a return to traditional nuclear family roles and values for white middle-class women. A contraction of the economy beginning in the early 1970s was accompanied by widespread acceptance of the goals of *women's liberation* movements that had formed during the 1960s. The large majority of American women, irrespective of race or ethnicity, now expect that they and their daughters will need to work outside the home to contribute to family support or that they will have to support themselves. They also expect that biological sex will not be a barrier to a fulfilling occupation. Law and public policy have supported those expectations, for instance, in greater access to higher education for women since the 1960s.

However, even in this generally liberatory climate for women, feminists of color perceive a need to define their problems within *parameters* of specific race and ethnicity. This is partly a reaction to ongoing perceptions of white racism throughout American society. It is also due to the facts that, in comparison with white women, women of color generally are more likely to be single heads of household, have less educational certification, make less money, be employed in lower-level, nonprofessional jobs, and experience unemployment. A minority of Asian women have educational levels and professional occupations comparable with white women. Single status and marital disruption have been higher for black and Puerto Rican women than any other group, although all groups among women of color have experienced some increase in being heads of household during recent decades. They disproportionately make up a new class of poor that is disproportionately populated by women and children. It should be noted nonetheless that increases in divorce and illegitimacy among all American women results in a white numerical majority of female heads of household in poverty.

Some black feminists, out of concern for problems caused by racism against black males, have deferred addressing the oppression of black women by black men.

These writers believe that for nonwhite women generally, racial oppression is more serious than gender oppression; they tend to think that white women are not as oppressed due to gender as all nonwhites are due to race. Some Native American feminists have emphasized the **matriarchal** political structures of traditional Indian cultures as well as Indigenist beliefs that male and female genders ought to have equal power in human society. These writers have insisted that traditional Native American women already were liberated before the European invasion. The task of contemporary Indian feminists is therefore Indian liberation generally, through a return to traditional tribal cultural structures. Other feminists of color demand immediate liberatory measures and recognition for themselves as black women, Latinas, Chicanas, Asian women, Indian women, mixed-race women, and so forth.

Some of the demands for recognition and empowerment of nonwhite women have been forcefully made by feminists of color who describe and criticize contemporary society from the standpoint of **lesbian** experience. As lesbians, they are able to place the lives and perspectives of women in the center of human experience. Not all lesbians center female experience on the basis of same-sex sexual preference. Some lesbians of color are women-oriented because they derive strength for overcoming disadvantage and resisting racism from other nonwhite female relatives and friends.

Some black women who have found inspiration as well as practical examples in the lives of their mothers and grandmothers have identified themselves as **womanists** since the 1980s. Many womanists are activists who emphasize the spiritual and social role of churches in black liberation. White feminists, by contrast, have often dismissed church activities on the grounds that organized religion is merely another oppressive dimension of patriarchy.

While few feminists of color claim to have a **grand theory** for universal human liberation, many feel that the particularly difficult intersections of race and gender that they experience make it necessary for them to create their knowledge based on their own experience. That is, they deliberately construct themselves as the only intellectuals who are qualified to analyze and change their own experience. Some believe that this intellectual authority can be used to liberate white women, men of color, and even some white men. If solutions to problems of people in the most difficult situations with the most marginalized identities can be found, then those solutions might apply to others who are, in terms of intersection, at least, less oppressed. That is, the reasoning would be, "If *I* could do it, anyone could do it."

D. DISCUSSION QUESTIONS

1. Discuss some instances in which people confuse social role differences between men and women with biological differences.

2. Is the disproportionate number of black males in the criminal justice system related to differences in black male gender in your opinion?

3. Have you or anyone you know experienced the limitations of a gender role that has been assigned on the grounds of race or ethnicity?

4. Can you think of any aspects of male or female gender that are not conditioned by race? Be as specific as possible.

5. If you were a black female college student who wanted to become a surgeon, would you be more concerned about barriers due to race or gender?

E. RECOMMENDED READING

For analyses of gender before the eighteenth century, see Merry E. Weisner, *Women and Gender in Early Modern Europe,* and Naomi Zack, *Bachelors of Science: Seventeenth Century Identity, Then and Now,* chapters 4 and 12.

For discussions of black male gender, see: Leonard Harris, "Honor: Emasculation and Empowerment," in Larry May and Robert A. Strikwerder, eds., *Rethinking Masculinity: Philosophical Explorations in Light of Feminism;* Waldo E. Martin, Jr., *The Mind of Frederick Douglass;* John P. Pittman, "Malcolm X: Masculinist Practice and Queer Theory," in Naomi Zack, ed., *RACE/SEX.* On occupational stereotypes and gender and race, see Judith Bradford and Crispin Sartwell, "Voiced Bodies/Embodied Voices," also in *RACE/SEX.*

For feminist psychological treatments of gender relative to race, see L. S. Brown and M. P. P. Root, eds., *Diversity and Complexity in Feminist Therapy.* See also, Ruben Martinez and Richard L. Dukes, "Ethnic and Gender Differences in Self Esteem," in *Youth and Society,* and Richard L. Dukes and Ruben Martinez, "The Impact of Ethgender Among Adolescence," in *Adolescence.* On feminist issues of essentialism, see: Judith Butler, *Gender Trouble: Feminism and the Subversion of Identity,* and Nancy Holmstrom, "Do Women Have a Distinct Nature?" in Marjorie Pearsall, ed., *Women and Values: Readings in Recent Feminist Philosophy.*

For an account of the history of black and white feminism as political movements, see Eleanor Flexner, *A Century of Struggle.* Issues involved in the intersection of blackness and female gender are analyzed by Kimberly Crenshaw, in "Demarginalizing the Intersection of Race and Sex: A Black Feminist Critique of Antidiscrimination Doctrine, Feminist Theory, and Antiracist Politics," in Alison Jagger, ed., *Living with Contradictions: Controversies in Feminist Social Ethics.* This intersection is explored in reference to Asian women by Karen Hossfeld in "Hiring Immigrant Women: Silicon Valley's 'Simple Formula'," in Maxine Baca Zinn and Bonnie Thornton Dill, eds., *Women of Color in U.S. Society.*

A comprehensive source for black women's studies is Darlene Clark Hine, *Black Women in America: An Historical Encyclopedia,* 2 vols. Contemporary black feminist issues are discussed in the following sources: Patricia Hill Collins, "Learning to Think for Ourselves: Malcolm X's Black Nationalism Reconsidered," in Joe Wood, ed., *Malcolm X: In Our Own Image,* and Collins, *Black Feminist Thought;* Shirley M. Geiger, "African-American Single Mothers: Public Perceptions and Public Policies," in Kim Marie Vaz, ed., *Black Women in America;* Paula Giddings, *When and Where I Enter: The Impact of Black Women on Race and Sex in America;* B. A. Greene, "What Has Gone Before: The Legacy of Racism and Sexism in the Lives of Black Mothers and Daughters," in L. S. Brown and M. P. P. Root, eds., *Di-*

versity and Complexity in Feminist Therapy; bell hooks, *Ain't I A Woman: Black Women and Feminism,* and *Feminist Theory: From Margin to Center,* as well as, "Sisterhood: Political Solidarity between Women," in Janet Kourany, James Sterba, and Rosemarie Tong, eds., *Feminist Philosophies;* Gloria T. Hull, et al., eds., *All the Women are White, all the Blacks are Men, But Some of Us are Brave: Black Women's Studies;* Audre Lorde, *Sister Outsider;* Peggy McIntosh, "White Privilege and Male Privilege: A Personal Account of Coming to See Correspondences Through Work in Women's Studies," in Anne Minas, ed., *Gender Basics.*

An historical presentation of different ideals of white womanhood, written before the current wave of feminism, is Emily James Putnam's *The Lady: Studies of Certain Significant Phases of Her History.*

For a nonfeminist black perspective on concerns shared by black Americans, see Nathan and Julia Hare, *The Endangered Black Family.* On womanism, see Alice Walker's *In Search of Our Mothers' Gardens.* On women and poverty, see Ruth Sidel, *Women and Children Last: The Plight of Poor Women in Affluent America.*

For feminist consideration of the situations of Indian and Asian Americans, see: Paula Gunn Allen, *The Sacred Hoop: Recovering the Feminine in American Indian Traditions;* C. K. Bradshaw, "Beauty and the Beast: On Racial Ambiguity," in Maria P. P. Root, ed., *Racially Mixed People in America;* Bonnie Thornton Dill, "Fictive Kin, Paper Sons, and *Compadrazgo:* Women of Color and the Struggle for Family Survival," in Zinn and Dill, eds., *Women of Color in U.S. Society;* Amy Ling, *Between Worlds: Women Writers of Chinese Ancestry;* Evelyn P. Stevens, "Marianismo: The Other Face of Machismo in Latin America," in Anne Minas, ed., *Gender Basics.* See also Curtis Chin, *Witness Aloud: Lesbian, Gay and Bisexual Asian/Pacific American Writing.*

SUPPOSE YOU ARE CLOSE FRIENDS WITH A PERSON OF A DIFFERENT
RACE WHO COULD BE A ROMANTIC PARTNER FOR YOU. BUT
DURING YOUR FRIENDSHIP, YOU HAVE EACH BEEN INVOLVED WITH
OTHER PEOPLE. HOWEVER, A TIME COMES WHEN YOU ARE BOTH
UNATTACHED AND YOUR FRIEND EXPRESSES A ROMANTIC INTEREST IN
YOU FOR THE FIRST TIME. BECAUSE YOU KNOW EACH OTHER WELL, YOU
ASK WHY THE CHANGE. "WELL," YOUR FRIEND ANSWERS, "I WONDERED
WHAT IT WOULD BE LIKE, YOU KNOW, WITH THE DIFFERENCE IN RACE."
HOW WOULD YOU REACT TO THIS ANSWER?

CHAPTER 10

RACE, ROMANCE, AND SEXUALITY

INTRODUCTION

There is a broad *folk model* of human sexuality in American culture which looks
something like this. Human sexuality is a natural drive or set of desires that propels
individuals toward sexual experiences with the opposite sex. These experiences are
intensely pleasurable to both sexes but especially to men, and the primary sexual experience is intercourse. The *naturalness* of this sex drive is obvious because it is necessary for the reproduction of our species and can be observed throughout the
biological kingdom, even in plants. *Notice that this model equates sex with heterosexuality and that it leaves love out of the picture.*

But there is a broad folk model for love as well: Falling in love is an exciting,
almost hypnotic experience that is usually connected with strong sexual desire for the
love object. If the bond of love is mutual and the pair have enough in common, and
they are able to do so, then they should get married, have children, talk about their
problems, raise their children, grow old together, and remain sexually faithful to one
another throughout this life. *Notice that this model associates heterosexuality with romantic love and that it leaves money out of the picture.*

There is no broad model for homosexual love but there is a model for the importance of money. Money is important but it is not as important as the well-being of
one's family. Therefore, couples should work hard, save their money so they can buy
a house, make more money, buy everything they need for the family, and set aside
enough money so their children can go to college and duplicate the same lifestyle, or
better yet, exceed it.

All three models work together as a simplified picture of what is normal and comes naturally, and as banal as these models appear, they have a powerful grip on the American psyche. As unifying ideals, there is nothing wrong with these models, but as descriptions of how human beings are, they omit the socially constructed aspects of both sexuality and romantic love and fail to take the social constructions of racial difference into account. The impact of racial difference on love and sex may make the combination of all three models more difficult to attain for some groups than others.

The way that adults present themselves sexually and develop and express their sexual desires is a complex result of social, individual, and biological processes that begin in childhood: physical and psychological development, personal inclination, family influence, peer interaction, education, media images, advertising, and income. Sexuality may *seem* natural but it is in fact highly influenced, if not structured, by changing cultural circumstances.

Even if there were a universal *sex drive* in human beings, that drive is never evident in what could be called a pure form. Sexual practices, sexual morality, and sexual choices vary widely from one culture to the next and over time within the same culture. Many external physical and social circumstances of human life, as well as individual desire and choice, determine the ways in which sexuality is experienced and expressed. It is therefore not surprising that race should intersect with sexuality as it does with gender. One obvious aspect of the intersection between sexuality and race is that the vast majority of Americans choose sexual partners who are of the same race that they are. Related to that pervasive fact is the existence of myths about nonwhite sexuality and sexual stereotypes of nonwhites. The purpose of this chapter is to examine some of the myths and stereotypes of nonwhite love and sexuality that are created and re-created in popular culture. Section A is an analysis of the methodology of contemporary cultural criticism that uses novels, movies, and other pop cultural products as evidence for deep beliefs in the culture. Section B is a comparative discussion of romantic and sexual stereotypes of white and nonwhite men in the movies. Section C is a comparative discussion of romantic and sexual stereotypes of white and nonwhite women in the movies. There are, of course, many other cultural sources and expressions of such stereotypes besides movies, for instance, print media, television, literature, theatre, visual arts, popular fiction and nonfiction, advertising, and music. The advantage of focusing on movies is that they are accessible to both audiences and critics. Their popular consumption means that they gratify and influence large numbers of people. As material objects, movies are cultural documents that can be repeatedly experienced, which means that they can be studied systematically. Also, insofar as racial identification depends largely on visual appearance, movies literally show everyone what members of different races and ethnicities look like.

A. ANALYSIS OF A CRITICAL METHOD

Contemporary cultural critics who interpret media, novels, and big news stories seem to share a common method in showing how people are *stereotyped* and describing the *myths* about how stereotyped people behave and fare in life. The method is to describe how types of people and events are depicted in the example of the medium in question. This description is then generalized as a statement of how the filmmaker and audience, or novelist and reader, or journalist and readers (etc.), perceive all members of the type to which the character belongs. And the generalization is then critically examined for bias, that is, racism, sexism, and classism. For example, suppose a black woman in a movie plays the role of a sexually provocative maid who is raped and then commits suicide. A critic using this method might claim that the movie presents an image of black women as irrational menial workers who can be victimized and who will react self-destructively to such victimization. As a generalization about black women, the movie depiction and events could be interpreted as racist, sexist, and classist.

There seem to be several assumptions behind this critical method. First, the critic assumes that the creators of every artistic product think that their product will be viewed, heard, or read as a universal description of social reality. If the creators did not intend for their work to be accepted as universal, then they could not be held socially responsible for how they present characters who are members of specific groups. A second assumption behind such criticism is that the audience is willing to accept what the creators intend to portray as universally true. For example, they observe the plight of the maid as though she were an *archetype* rather than a unique individual. If the audience didn't believe that what they saw or read had this kind of general truth, the critical method based on generalization would be pointless. Members of audiences are used to reacting to the real people they meet and interact with, as unique individuals, so why shouldn't they be expected to regard movie characters as particular individuals in the same way?

A response to this criticism of the critical method is that claims based on descriptions of events in popular cultural products need to have a wide empirical base in order to be valid. One movie in which a black woman is victimized is not sufficient to make a case about popular stereotypes about black women. But if over a period of time, all or most black female roles in movies that do well at the box office depict menials who are victimized, then the critical generalizations about stereotype and myth have some foundation. If the novel *Gone with the Wind* had a small cult following, not much about American nostalgia for the antebellum South could be asserted. But the novel is still outselling the Bible, there is a well-attended theme park built around a "reproduction" of Scarlet O'Hara's ancestral plantation, Tara, in Georgia, and deluxe collectible editions of videos of the movie *Gone with the Wind* sell well. Thus conclusions about wide-scale stereotypes and myths would seem to be in order.

The critical method of examining stereotypes and myths through popular art further assumes that people look to film and other media to see what they already believe and to have those beliefs further articulated and strengthened. It is through the further articulation and strengthening process that the media may keep stereotypes and myths alive, teach them to upcoming generations, and bring them up-to-date in a rapidly changing society. That is, as the media continually reach out to give the public what it wants, and the public reaches out to its media to find out what it wants, they form a partnership of creating and re-creating stereotypes and myths. While this process does not affect independent thinkers who are always vigilant and reluctant to suspend their disbelief, it does create a shared consensus about what other people think. For example, if there is a popular myth that young black males are predatory criminals, a white-on-white crime victim who wants sympathy but does not want to reveal the identity of the perpetrator, may tell authorities that a black man did it.

B. ROMANTIC AND SEXUAL MOVIE STEREOTYPES OF MEN, BY RACE

Let's begin with romantic and sexual stereotypes of white males. First, it is striking that the romantic sexual desirability of northern European males is not a traditional basis for primary typing as it is, for example, with "Latin lovers." Therefore, strictly speaking, there are no white male romantic and sexual stereotypes. Rather, white males are portrayed as having nonromantic and nonsexual qualities that women find attractive, such as good looks, physical and psychological strength, heroism, decisiveness, courage, talent, power, and so on. There are two ways to interpret this. The first is that white males have reserved normal masculine humanity for themselves, in a culture in which they dominate. The second is that white males as a group are romantically and sexually repressed.

The theory of white male repression is connected to a causal theory of the exaggerated eroticism of nonwhite males. As the result of a work ethic and moral traditions that do not consider love and sex important (in comparison to money, knowledge, and power), white males project the erotic side of their psyches onto males of nonwhite racial groups. The nonwhite males, once mythologized as exaggeratedly erotic, are envied, feared, and hated by white males. At the same time, their exaggerated eroticism disqualifies nonwhite males from playing major roles connected to the serious concerns of life, such as business, science, political leadership, and military might.

In movies, racial divisions seem to be drawn so that the privileges of white masculinity are conferred mainly on northern Europeans. As the men get more southern in European geography, they tend to be portrayed as more interested in romance and sex. Another way of putting this is that masculine sexuality is cinematically depicted on a quantitative continuum from white to black skin. Thus, masculine sexuality increases as masculine gender power decreases. To a lesser extent, it also works the other way: masculine sexuality decreases as masculine gender power increases. Insofar as masculine sexuality is associated with heterosexuality, the "whiter" the man is, the more subject to portrayal as effeminate or sissified, as in stereotypes of the English homosexual dandy. Similarly, the "blacker" the man is, the more is he subject to portrayal as a sexual predator, as in the stereotype of the African American rapist.

The sexual and romantic stereotypes of black males cluster around the attributes of large physical size, romantic infidelity, expertise in lovemaking, and emotional and physical abuse of female sexual objects of all races. It is rare for a serious love relationship between a man and a woman to be depicted with a black male protagonist or hero. Beyond sex, black men are stereotyped as romantically irresponsible or comical. The dutiful and supportive black husband is either a cardboard figure

in popular entertainment, or a comedian. One asset of the way black men are stereotyped in American popular entertainment is that in the context of what would have to
be called a *homophobic* masculine culture, generally, they are rarely portrayed as
homosexuals.

While Hispanics are officially classified as an ethnicity rather than a race, their
romantic and sexual portrayals differ from white male stereotypes. Hispanic men
tend to be stereotyped as "ladies' men," men who are very knowledgeable about the
sensibilities and needs of women. They are frequently depicted in movies as fickle
and unfaithful, emotionally superficial, and often financially as well as emotionally
exploitative of women. Thus, the other side of *Don Juan,* who knows how to "really
love a woman," is that he knows how to really leave a woman (with a broken heart).
The stereotype is not monolithic, however, because Mexican men are often depicted
as stalwart family men.

While Italians are white in all designations of race in American culture, they
are depicted with more intense interest in romance and sex than northern European
men. Jewish men, by contrast, who are also now officially designated white, are not
given roles as romantically serious as those assigned to other white ethnicities; instead, a strong humorous dimension seems to be consistently added to their sexuality
which is not present in the sexual depictions of men in other racial and ethnic groups.
The positive aspect of such comedy is that it allows for wit, which is rare in movie
depictions of romance today. But the negative connotation is that Jewish men are not
as masculine as men from other racial and ethnic groups.

Although Asian men frequently star in martial arts movies, they are rarely cast
as sexual and romantic figures. When they do appear in such roles, they are likely to
be portrayed as perverse or degenerate if young or middle-aged. As elders, they are
often visible as ancient patriarchs, benign and wise grandfathers well removed from
the erotic fray.

American Indian men, while they are stereotyped as either impossibly noble
and heroic, or violently out of control, are rarely portrayed in romantic contexts. It's
not immediately clear why this is so except that current popular images of Indians
generally run to the ethereal and near-extinct. Older images of Indians in westerns
depicted them as "bloodthirsty savages," cruel scalpers and rapists whose actions on
screen were meant to justify their massacre by white soldiers and cowboys.

Men who are racially mixed in appearance tend to be romantically and sexually
typed in the direction of the race that they most closely resemble. If the man's racial
mixture is part of the story line, that is, if anything is said about it, a tragic end is
likely for that character, regardless of the race of the woman who is his romantic
counterpart.

Arabs appear to be the one male group that can be portrayed as engaging in homosexual activity without distortions in their masculinity or moral character. Sometimes this seems to reflect a deference to a perceived acceptance of homosexuality in
Arab cultures, which would make the depiction of homosexuality among Arabs a
kind of time-out in American homophobia. The alternative interpretation is that such
depictions are the only ways in which moviemakers can show homosexual relationships to American audiences without offense, because being foreign makes them less
likely to be identified with by American men.

There is a sharp color line in cinematic depictions of sex and romance. Black men can be paired with black, Asian, mixed-black, Native American, East Indian, and dark-skinned Hispanic women without it being perceived necessary to present the racial difference as a problem. Black men cannot be paired with white women unless the racial difference is one of the subjects of the movie. Such black-white pairings, which were historically taboo and resulted in violence against black men, do not result in the cinematic pair living happily ever after.

C. ROMANTIC AND SEXUAL MOVIE STEREOTYPES OF WOMEN, BY RACE

First, unlike white males, white women are erotically stereotyped in American movies and not any kind of white woman can be depicted in a sexual role. White women have to be within child-bearing years and relatively thin in order to be cast in romantic and sexual roles that will attract large audiences. The romantic and sexual behavior of women in movies follows from their social or occupational roles. Thus, if a woman is someone's wife, her sexuality is likely to be subdued on screen—unless she is committing adultery, which takes her out of her wifely role. Mothers are rarely depicted in sexually exciting situations unless they are unfit mothers or unusually attractive. If a woman has a service job such as waitress, nurse, or secretary, she is likely to be portrayed as supportive and nurturing of the man with whom she is romantically or sexually involved. Professional or artistic women are less predictable romantically and sexually; although they are allowed to have intense and selfish, romantic and sexual interests, their male partners are often harmed by them, suggesting that independent women are dangerous to men. Prostitutes are portrayed as the most sexual of working women, but also the most unsuitable romantically from masculine points of view. Lesbians have become cinematic characters in recent years but in order to be of interest to broad audiences, they have to look as though they would be sexually and romantically interesting to heterosexual men, that is, be nubile and thin.

Generally, all women in romantic and sexual roles, regardless of race or ethnicity, are portrayed in movies from the perspective of male heterosexual viewers. Even in movies made for predominantly female audiences, female romantic and sexual characters are supposed to look sexually attractive to men. Male romantic leads, by contrast, do not have to be presented as sexually attractive to women by virtue of any special traits such as youth or thinness. They are presumed to be of romantic and sexual interest to women simply by being placed in romantic and sexual contexts. This suggests that for a man to be a romantic and sexual character it is enough if other men can identify with him, whereas the ability of women to have other women identify with them is not enough to certify their desirability. Another way of describing this situation is that in the movies, women are still the *sexual objects,* in the sense of chosen recipients, rather than the *sexual subjects,* in the sense of those who do the choosing. As subjects, men can be young, old, fat, thin, handsome, ugly, healthy, ill—it doesn't matter. But as objects, women have to conform to prevailing conventions and fashions—not just any object will do.

Although women are the chosen romantic and sexual objects in movies, there are still limitations on who may choose them. White women may be chosen by white men only. When nonwhite men choose them, an issue has to be made of this fact and the relationship is not likely to have a happy ending. Nonwhite women may be chosen by men of any race, especially for casual sexual liaisons. In serious relationships on screen, especially marriage, nonwhite women are most likely to be chosen by men of the same race.

While there are increasing roles for nonwhite women in the same range of occupations that are available to white women, as romantic and sexual objects nonwhite women tend to be wives, girlfriends, entertainers, seductresses, and prostitutes. While television shows and movies abound with black female judges in short courtroom scenes, and one does see nonwhite female doctors and lawyers with increasing frequency, the combination of these professional occupations with romantic and sexual appeal is rare. This suggests a general stereotype of either low socioeconomic class or a lack of intellectual talent in nonwhite women. One way to interpret this is that since women are generally at a disadvantage to men and nonwhites at a disadvantage to whites, it is just highly unlikely for nonwhite women to be accepted as professionals in the mass mind. But, as already noted, professional roles for nonwhite women are increasing in cinema, so that cannot be the full reason. More likely, the exaggerated sexuality that is assigned to nonwhite women is assumed to be incompatible with intelligence. Thus, in the movies, sexuality intersects with gender and race to create yet another restriction for nonwhite women, this time one of intellect. However, the stereotype of the (white) "dumb blonde" suggests that the association of stupidity with sexiness goes beyond race.

There is a rich variety of moral vice that seems to accompany the depiction of nonwhite female romantic characters. Black and Hispanic women are often portrayed as hysterical, physically violent, materialistic, superficial, promiscuous, vain, and unfaithful. Self-indulgence is another vice, especially in the consumption of alcohol and drugs. Nonwhite women are frequently depicted as prostitutes in ways that do not require any special explanation as to how or why they became prostitutes in the first place. In contrast, white prostitutes quite often have other morally redeeming qualities, and they are expected to explain how they became prostitutes.

Generally, the self-destructive aspect of the moral vices that are ascribed to black, Hispanic, and Asian female romantic characters contribute to a sexually alluring masochism, rather than evident self-destructiveness that is a call for help. Their pain itself may be objectified as a sexually stimulating attribute. When they are not prostitutes, black and Hispanic women are often portrayed as aggressive and shameless in initiating sex with men. Asian women, however, are often idealized as traditional sexual objects on cinema. They are depicted as compliant to the wishes of men, generally subdued in affect, noncompetitive, and sexually submissive and seductive.

As with men in romantic and sexual roles, Jewish and Italian women, while considered white in the culture, are depicted differently on screen from northern European white women. Both Jewish and Italian women are presented as more sexual types than northern European women, more aggressive sexually and more interested in sex. However, as with Jewish men, the general sexual and romantic sensibility of

Jewish women is often portrayed in ways that cast doubt on their conformity to traditional ideals of white female gender. Thus, Jewish women in romantic leads are stereotyped as overly talkative, critical, and generally not submissive to men.

Similar to portrayals of masculine sexuality, there is a cinematic color line from white to black skin, along which the intensity of female sexuality varies. If this is due to a suppression of sexuality in northern European women, to match the repression of sexuality in northern European men, it allows for a sublimation of sexuality into romance for northern European women. Not surprisingly, white northern European couples are the cinematic prototype for couples who fall in love, marry, have children, buy houses, and so on.

The more intense sexualization of darker-skinned women is not a neutral fact. As sexual rather than romantic objects, these women are portrayed on screen as being unusually attractive to men. They can be viewed either as outlets for repressed sexuality or, in conjunction with their cinematic moral vices, as symbols of what has in European Christian culture been constructed as the dark, sinful side of the human psyche. Thus, parallel to the male white-black continuum with an English sissy on one end and a black rapist on the other, the female white-black continuum runs from frigid northern European women (including nuns) to oversexed black women (including prostitutes and other sinners who are "beyond rape.") Most rape victims are played by white women. Until recently, in reality as well as cinema, rapists whose victims were black women (and children) were not prosecuted, particularly if the rapists were white.

The one exception to the more intense sexuality projected onto nonwhite women in the movies sometimes occurs with Native American female romantic leads. While presented as matter-of-fact and "natural" about sex, Native American women are not depicted as sinful sexual beings. Rather, they are mythologized as ethical beings with strong spiritual values that derive from a privileged racial connection to the earth. They are the angels of current cinematic conceit, not of this world insofar as it is artificial and corrupt and capable of leading men, especially white men, to a better place. Real Indian women with contemporary problems of work, family, and health are not portrayed as romantic and sexual characters on screen.

D. DISCUSSION QUESTIONS

1. Describe, in as much detail as you can, a sexual stereotype attached to a man or woman of a particular nonwhite race.

2. Describe a sexual stereotype attached to a man or woman of mixed race.

3. Describe in detail how a movie or TV show you are familiar with reinforces a racial sexual stereotype. Or, describe one that breaks a stereotype.

4. Do you think people acquire racial sexual stereotypes from the movies? If so, what would the psychological process be?

5. What racial sexual stereotypes do nonwhites have about whites?

E. RECOMMENDED SOURCES

Film

Recent portrayals of white men as nonsexual but nonetheless sexually attractive types are ubiquitous. See, for example, *Unforgiven, The American President, Mr. Holland's Opus,* and *Sabrina,* not to mention any one of probably thousands of action movies.

In the early days of American theater, in the genre of **minstrelsy,** blacks did not appear on stage and their parts were played by whites in "blackface." Until the late 1960s, serious black characters were rare on screen. A traditional stereotype of both romantic stage and screen has been the tragic mulatto, usually an attractive mixed-race woman who looks white but cannot achieve happiness in love with a white man due to her black ancestry. This figure can be traced through *Showboat, Imitation of Life,* and most recently, *Devil in a Blue Dress.* Mixed-race men are also depicted as alienated tragic figures. See: *Invitation to a Gunfight,* and more recently, *Map of the Human Heart.*

Even superficial interracial romantic relationships are generally doomed in movies. When the man is black and the woman is white, often lurid tragedy results, as in *A Native Son,* or the outcome is frustration and misunderstanding, as in *Jungle Fever.* The sinister side of interracial sex in American life has been the lynching and castration of black men believed to have white female partners and the sexual exploitation and rape of black women by white men. The overt racism that swirls around these situations is depicted in the movies *Rosewood* and *A Time to Kill.*

Such portrayals of interracial sex draw on broader myths about the sexuality of black men and women. Black men tend to be portrayed as romantically and sexually irresponsible, as, for instance, the black heroines of *Waiting to Exhale* lament. Black women are supposed to be highly interested in sex but even more interested in money, as the same movie attests. In contrast, the white heroines of *First Wives Club* are more interested in self-fulfillment. Other portrayals of black women emphasize their tribulations and sorrows, with success and happiness small blips at the end if the heroine overcomes adversity, as in *What's Love Got to Do with It?* Sometimes, real-life tragedy converges with art, as in *Lady Day: The Many Faces of Billie Holliday.*

There is little in film portrayals of romantic love between black men and women that is not based on sex and money. Powerful emotional and ethical conflicts seem to be reserved for white characters. The subplot of emotional tension between the black married couple in *Courage Under Fire* is resolved only when the black protagonist solves his problems concerning courage involving white people. Homosexuality is portrayed with even less frequency than it is with white characters, except for small independent efforts, such as the film *Paris is Burning* that documents black and Hispanic men in female drag. Black lesbianism is presented in a counter-culture type of fantasy in *The Color Purple.*

A male Latin lover stereotype [Antonio Banderas] can be found in *Too Much.* Many of Woody Allen's movies capitalize on the "off-center" stereotype of male Jewish masculinity. See also, *Portnoy's Complaint.* Barbara Streisand's roles do the same with Jewish femininity. The animated film *Pocahontas* presents the female Native American spiritual stereotype. See Frederic Mitterand's 1995 version of *Madame Butterfly* for a depiction of Asian female passivity. In the 1992 movie *The Last of His Tribe,* the genocide of the Washo Indians in central California is dramatized by the alienation and enforced sexual loneliness of their last survivor in 1911.

Media Events and Sex and Race

In recent years, the American public has weathered at least three major media storms concerning the alleged dangerous sexuality of black men: Mike Tyson's rape trial, Clarence Thomas's Supreme Court nomination hearings, and the O. J. Simpson trial. (In addition, as of this writing, cases are pending involving sexual misconduct by black officers in the military.) Most Americans believe that Mike Tyson was guilty of rape, Clarence Thomas of sexual harassment, and O. J. Simpson of murder. Whether these judgments are correct or not, they reinforce negative stereotypes and myths. As popular as Colin Powell may have been for a while, his achievements did not have the same degree of audience interest as the sexual misconduct of the other men.

Marlon Riggs discusses portrayals of black male sexuality on television in "Sexuality, Television, and Death: A Black Gay Dialogue on Malcolm X," in Joe Wood, ed., *Malcolm X: In Our Own Image.* Bridget Freydberg chronicles roles played by black and Hispanic women in older movies, in "Sapphires, Spitfires, Sluts and Superbitches: Aframericans and Latinas in Contemporary American Film," in Kim Marie Vaz, ed., *Black Women in America.*

There have been no recent media events featuring black women that have compared to the scandals involving black men, with the exception of the vilification of Anita Hill who testified against Clarence Thomas. See Toni Morrison, ed., *Race-ing Justice, En-gendering Power: Essays on Anita Hill, Clarence Thomas and the Construction of Social Reality,* on this case.

Readings on interracial sexual relations include: Beth Day, *Sexual Life Between Blacks and Whites: The Roots of Racism;* L. R. Tenzer, *A Completely New Look at Interracial Sexuality: Public Opinion and Select Commentaries;* I. Stuart and L. Abt, eds., *Interracial Marriage: Expectations and Realities.* (There is also a current film, *Mr. and Mrs. Loving,* about the couple who brought the lawsuit that resulted in the U.S. Supreme Court striking down existing anti-miscegenation laws in 1967.) See also: Calvin Hernton, *Sex and Racism in America.*

Thomas Laquer presents an historical analysis of the relationship between sex and gender in *Making Sex: Body and Gender from the Greeks to Freud.* Lawrence Stone offers an historical account of early modern sexuality in *The Family, Sex and Marriage in England, 1500–1800.*

Toni Morrison's novel *The Bluest Eye* explores the effects on black women of ideals of white female sexuality. Laurie Shrage examines the fact that the majority of working prostitutes worldwide are nonwhite in *Moral Dilemmas of Feminism: Prostitution, Adultery and Abortion,* chapter 6.

For contemporary philosophical analyses of social constructions of nonwhite sexuality, see the following, all in Naomi Zack, ed., *RACE/SEX:* Lewis R. Gordon, "Race, Sex and Matrices of Desire in an Antiblack World"; Kevin Thomas Miles,

"Body Badges: Race and Sex"; Naomi Zack, "The American Sexualization of Race." See also, L. Jones, *Bulletproof Diva: Tales of Race, Sex, and Hair.*

For international analyses of nonwhite homosexuality, see Anne McClintock, Jose Esteban Muñoz and Trish Rosen, eds., *Race and Queer Sexuality.* See also: Gina Machetti, *Romance and 'The Yellow Peril': Race, Sex and Discoursive Strategies in Hollywood Fiction;* Russell Leong, *Asian American Sexualities: Dimensions of the Gay and Lesbian Experience;* Åsebrit Sundquist, *Pocahontas & Co.: The Fictional American Indian Woman in Nineteenth-Century Literature: A Study of Method;* Ward Churchill (M. Annette Jaimes, ed.), *Fantasies of the Master Race.*

CHAPTER 11

RACE AND CLASS

INTRODUCTION

A classless, egalitarian society has long been an American ideal, especially in the Western states. The ideal is that regardless of origins, everyone is equal in the eyes of the law; all have the same opportunities for material success and the same rights to respect and privacy from others. Throughout the nineteenth century, it was popularly believed that privilege and snobbery were symptoms of European decadence and corruption. Americans were all equal as part of their constitutional rights as individuals, their spirit of independence, and their shared sense of being part of a young, dynamic civilization. A system of *social caste,* with unchanging hereditary membership on each level of a hierarchy of social status and economic and political power, was deeply repugnant to the majority of Americans. This idealistic aversion to class and caste has been reinforced in practice by the continuously changing nature of American culture. Americans have never had a strong, broad sense of the importance of history. The past is something vaguely behind us that we constantly shed, even though we nostalgically reinvent selected parts of it.

Serious knowledge of the past, and attachment to *tradition* simply because it is tradition, are important components of class and caste systems. Therefore, the lack of a strong sense of history is part of the American aversion to class and caste. Nonetheless, this aversion is not the same thing as an actual absence of class and caste. Since colonial days, there have been inherited divisions between rich and poor, powerful and disenfranchised. While Americans do not make rigid personal or moral judgments about preferred family backgrounds and *breeding,* education and income are still great social dividers.

Men from established, prestigious families, who are also graduates of a handful of exclusive preparatory schools and universities, have occupied the highest political, business, and institutional positions in this country since the nineteenth century. In parallel ways, their mothers, sisters, and wives have been occupied in charities, formal social events, and support for the arts. This ruling elite marries within its own ranks and is the unacknowledged American upper class. Members of the vast middle class (or classes) below it range from affluent professionals to skilled blue-collar workers and small business proprietors. Below the middle class are the poor: employed unskilled workers, and the occasionally unemployed. At the bottom is an underclass: clients of welfare, the homeless, seasonal workers, the chronically unemployed, petty criminals who work the streets, and blue-collar criminals in prison, awaiting trial, or on probation.

While the different socioeconomic levels are generally acknowledged, most Americans hesitate to call them a class system for two reasons. First, it is believed that opportunity exists on every level for those who are hard working and enterprising. Second, many groups and individuals have moved up socioeconomically. Although a smaller number have moved down and there are always individuals moving down due to unemployment, these cases are not considered typical.

It should be remembered that despite upward mobility, adults on every socioeconomic level have children who automatically start out as members of the class to which their parents belong. Also, as the socioeconomic levels get lower, so do the moral appraisals attached to them. Poverty itself is shameful in the United States. The very words "up" and "down," or "upper," "middle," and "lower" suggest that something more than variety is at stake with class difference.

In the United States, the mere possession of money has always had the power to provide security and respect for just about anyone. Historically, upward mobility through the unacknowledged class system has usually accompanied financial success. The archetypical immigrant success story begins with a first generation that works hard at whatever employment it can get. Parents in the first generation assist the second generation financially and encourage success in the educational system. The second generation sees the third generation achieve solid business or professional status and full social acceptance as American by the larger society.

The popular model of an American classless and casteless society breaks down against the limiting facts of poverty within the white group and the ongoing conditions of racial segregation and discrimination within each class. Just as race intersects with gender and sexuality, it also intersects with socioeconomic class. The issues involved in that intersection form the topics of this chapter. Section A is a discussion of *liberation theory* generally, and *class theory* in particular. Section B is a discussion of the relevance of socioeconomic and racial difference to childhood experience. Section C focuses directly on how social class intersects with race at this time in the United States.

A. LIBERATION THEORY AND CLASS THEORY

An *ideology* is a critical description and analysis of social reality that is motivated by a commitment to change some aspects of that reality. Unlike religion or theology, ideology has purely secular concerns and is usually formulated around the conditions and goals of a particular historical group. Communism, socialism, and capitalism are ideologies, as are feminism and black liberation. Over time, the scholarly development of ideologies results in *critical theories*. The ongoing gap between the ideological goals and reality is analyzed in terms of existing social structures that are not fully understood by their participants. The absence of justice and equality may be explained in terms of the interests of dominant groups that have unfair advantages, such as white men, white racists, profit-motivated business people, or power-motivated politicians. However, unless members of subordinate groups such as women, non-whites, consumers, and citizens, become aware of their positions as members of subordinate groups, liberatory social change is unlikely. Critical theorists usually offer their analyses in the service of such liberatory change.

There is a long tradition in Western culture of political ideologies based on theories of social classes. The ancient Greeks viewed social classes as political reflections of natural classes among human beings. They believed there was a *natural aristocracy* of morally and intellectually superior human beings. This natural aristocracy was assumed to consist of rich men of high social status who had a right to rule. The justification for this ancient *elitism* was, first, that it was believed right for the best to rule, and second, that everyone would benefit if the best ruled.

The European industrial revolution gave rise to a new middle class that worked hard for profit and accumulated material wealth as its reward. This capitalistic owning class had its own political theorists, who attacked the privileges of monarchs and nobles on the grounds that all men were equal. They argued that those men who had acquired material goods had a fundamental right to the enjoyment of their possessions and the freedom to acquire more; they were also entitled to political representation to protect their property rights. One part of the justification for capitalism and representative government was *natural law:* God had made men equal, decreed that they should work, and given them the power to construct social and legal systems that would protect their private property. The other part of the justification for capitalism and representative government was the claim that in the long run, all members of society would be better off and prosper if there were freedom for the enterprising to acquire wealth and keep it. Surplus wealth would support science and the arts, and provide charitable assistance to those who labored for subsistence without acquiring anything. Women were not originally part of the capitalistic system except as wives in the middle class and laborers among the working poor. The role of nonEuropeans, especially those from parts of the world that were colonized to use their raw materials in capitalistic production, was politically and socially *marginalized.*

During the nineteenth century, the third phase in Western European ideology about social class centered on the working class. It was at this stage that Karl Marx gave the critical theory of social and economic class its most radical liberatory form. According to Marx, all human beings had to work and produce or process material things to survive. Every human society had characteristic and dominant means of production, which in the nineteenth century were industrial enterprises such as factories and mines. The social class that controlled the dominant nineteenth-century means of production, and which was, through representative government, the effective ruling class, was the *bourgeoisie.* The bourgeoisie lived and ruled on the basis of the difference in the value of the goods produced by the workers or *proletariat,* and what it paid the proletariat in wages. This difference was the *profit* that motivated capitalists. The European proletariat was exploited because it was not paid enough to securely sustain life or develop personally in leisure time. Therefore, according to *Marxist ideology,* the proletariat ought to take over and run the means of production through which it already produced everything. Common ownership of the means of production by the workers through their government, or ***communism,*** was justified both on the grounds that it was morally right and that all classes in society would live more fulfilling lives as a result.

Within Western political ideology, the class posited as potentially liberatory for all thus shifted from the aristocracy in ancient times, to the middle class during the early modern period, to the working class in the late modern period. Of course, this shift marks the chronology of influential theories rather than popular belief. In the United States, for example, communism was never widely accepted as a political ideology and bourgeois ideology, or the ideology of capitalism, remains dominant.

As critical theories, both feminism and racial liberation also operate on the premises that the liberation of women and nonwhites is just, and that once these groups are liberated, everyone else will benefit. Many feminists believe that full equality for women will also entail full equality and more enriching lives for all men. Many black liberationists believe that full social equality for black people will also set white people free. In both cases, universal liberation is projected because situations of oppression are believed to waste energy and repress love, creativity, and personal freedom among oppressors and oppressed alike.

It is not merely the goods that accrue to individuals due to their social class position that are important for human happiness and fulfillment according to class theory. Rather, the nature of the work each class engages in and its relation to the means of production is crucial to human well-being. If people labor at boring, repetitive, and uncomfortable tasks, their work brings about feelings of alienation and personal emptiness. Even great wealth cannot buy human satisfaction in a culture that does not value creativity, play, and intellectual development. While the solution to poverty in a technologically complex society might be more money through gainful employment, this solution does not address the absence of nonmaterial satisfactions.

Some leading contemporary Native American critical theorists have rejected classic Marxist analyses as irrelevant to Indian liberatory struggles because they do not think that redistribution of wealth and employment would result in the human goods that they value. Within Indian cultures, natural environments themselves are believed to be more important than the consumer items produced from resources extracted from these environments. Therefore, both capitalism and communism are considered parts of the same unbalanced and unnatural cultural process. Indian identity and loyalty are expressed in relation to particular Indian nations (that non-Indians used to call tribes), which, if not externally interfered with by EuroAmericans, would continue in ways of living that are mutually beneficial to human beings and nature.

In contrast to those Native American critical theorists who believe that social class oppression is irrelevant to their fundamental concerns, some African American critical theorists have argued that high unemployment and poverty, rather than racism, is the fundamental cause of African American problems. These theorists contend that the civil rights legislation of the 1960s made it possible only for blacks who were already in positions to do so to rise socioeconomically. Since the mid-1960s, remedies for racism such as affirmative action programs, have not improved conditions for the majority of blacks, who remain poor and educationally disadvantaged. If anything, the gains afforded privileged blacks have divided the black community, especially after the new black middle class left the inner cities. Therefore, these critics propose that the way to solve the problems of the black urban poor is to create employment and educational opportunities directly for them, or encourage them to do so themselves.

B. Childhood, Class, and Race

The more complicated adult life is, the longer the period of childhood. Childhood is a variable chunk of human life without adult responsibility or obligation. In contemporary Western middle-class culture, childhood is supposed to be nurturing and enjoyable for children. Adults are supposed to take care of children, and the work of childhood is learning and play. This concept of childhood is not universal, either across cultures or historically. During the Middle Ages, eight was held to be the age of reason, and children were expected to be gainfully employed unless they belonged to leisured groups where adults did not work either. Child labor among the poor did not officially end in Western society until the early twentieth century, and many children throughout the world are still expected to earn their keep and contribute to family income.

There are varied theories about the influence of events in childhood on later life. The application of such theories to middle-class child rearing began in the late 1600s. It then became accepted among educated, progressive-minded parents in England and France that children ought to be taught through play and motivated by parental praise and blame rather than physical punishment. Thought was given to the practical content of educational curricula, to teach the sons of the bourgeoisie how to carry on the productive economic and civic responsibilities of their fathers.

Most middle-class parents today believe that they have an obligation to protect their children from the harsh realities of human life, indulge their desire for play, and refrain from corporal punishment whenever possible. They also agree that the serious business of parenting includes preparing children to become productive members of the middle class when they grow up.

Not only the virtues of child rearing but the virtues of children themselves have their base in middle-class values in the United States. Since the middle class is predominantly white, nonwhite and non-middle-class groups have different values to impart to children and they reinforce different virtues of childhood. Parents who do not have college educations or the financial and social resources, that is, the *leisure,* to teach their children how to behave like middle-class children are unlikely to *reproduce* middle-class values in the course of child rearing. Children of the poor are therefore likely to grow up with different values, different ideas of what is important in life, from middle-class children. If their parents have to deal with racism, children will learn antiracist strategies from those examples. Such defenses against racism may include a deliberate rejection of the activities at which only white people seem to excel, such as success in school. Neighborhood violence might cause fears about physical survival in childhood and make it seem as though having weapons and being prepared to fight are the best tactics for remaining alive. Without resources for play, alcohol and drug consumption and other high-risk behaviors may appear to be acceptable forms of recreation.

The children of migrant agricultural workers, who have to labor and grow up without a stable sense of place, also fail to experience the structures of childhood that are considered normal in the middle class, perhaps more so than any other group. If they are further denied access to public services, such as education and health care, their chances of living more advantaged lives than their parents are further reduced.

C. CLASS AND RACE

Most people grow up to belong to the same social class as their parents. Since nonwhite race is a limiting factor in upward social-class mobility, race works to reinforce the limitations that result from class and creates further sets of limitations for children of nonwhite races. Some writers have explained the social construction of race as a way to divide the American laboring class. It has already been noted in Chapter 6 that nonwhite race is a barrier to full access to middle- and upper-class advantages. This has resulted in nonwhites disproportionately remaining in the working class over generations.

Although members of the white working class have been exploited by white managers and entrepreneurs, the white working class has not always made strong demands for liberation on the grounds of working-class identity. It has been suggested that one reason for this is that white identity has been an implicit part of white working-class wages. The American union movement was successful in securing higher wages, health insurance, unemployment benefits, and the curtailment of child labor, but labor unions have traditionally had white majorities. To this day, many Hispanic workers in agriculture and Asian workers in low-tech assembly jobs are not unionized. Union workers tend to be skilled workers, who consider themselves middle class. Racial disparity in union membership and the lack of a strong working-class identity across racial difference have had a "whitening" effect on the successful segment of the American working class.

The middle class can be defined as the group that is able to attain and maintain the economic and social goals of home ownership, steady employment, college education, and more or less stable nuclear family life. Personal fulfillment and job satisfaction are most likely to be found in middle-class employment. Traditionally in American history, the middle class has been white, although it does have nonwhite members. However, black members of the middle class consistently do not do as well as their white counterparts: they make less money, own less property, and send fewer children to college; their health statistics are also not as favorable as those of whites. Asians and Jews are generally well established in the economic aspects of middle-class life. Hispanics do not generally have a strong presence in the middle class and Native Americans are barely visible there.

There are very few nonwhite members of the American upper class. Within the Asian American and black communities, there are socioeconomic class structures that in themselves have been based on racial or ethnic difference. For example, Vietnamese refugees occupy the lowest socioeconomic levels among Asians; newly arrived immigrants from China and Korea who did not have high socioeconomic status in their countries of origin do not have it in the United States when they start out in the workforce.

The African American community has contained socioeconomic division since colonial days. There were free blacks in the North and even in slave-owning states all through the period of slavery. Some were *freedmen* and their descendants, whereas others had never been enslaved. This group was never accepted by white society, but its members could own property and acquire literacy. Among enslaved blacks, those who were overseers, had domestic authority, or were owned by wealthy men were better off materially and had higher social status. The black members of the American middle class, especially those who have family traditions of college education and membership in the professions, have been an upper class within the black community.

Until the **Harlem Renaissance** of the 1930s, when African Americans generally began to unite as a racial group, there was an American **mulatto elite,** mixed race in ancestry and appearance, that had family histories of advanced education and professional employment (within the black community). Recognition of the white ancestry of this class contributed to its elevated social status, and its members were frequently selected by white leaders to be leaders of projects concerning blacks generally. This historical association of privilege and whiteness at times made the mulatto elite exceptionally unpopular with poor, uneducated blacks and their spokespersons. While the mulatto elite no longer exists, blacks who are successful in mainstream white society are still often resented by poor, undereducated blacks. It is a fact of capitalistic life for the poor to resent the rich, but within the black community this resentment carries the accusation of not being an authentic member of "the race."

In both urban and rural areas, black race has intersected with disadvantaged socioeconomic class to create a **black underclass** of hard-core unemployed and their children. As noted in Section B, the plight of the urban section of this class is viewed partly as the result of black middle-class flight from black urban neighborhoods to suburbs. The plight of the rural section is viewed partly as a general migration to cities by enterprising young people from depressed rural areas. More broadly, the existence of a black underclass is viewed as the most unfortunate result of institutionalized antiblack racism in the United States. Still, the demographic and racist background causes of this class do not prevent it from being feared and hated by other socioeconomic and racial groups in the culture. It is believed that the disproportionate number of black men who are involved in the criminal justice system are "bred" in female-headed households within the black urban underclass, and that the black urban underclass is the main "grassroots" support for illegal drug use and distribution in the United States today. The disadvantaged class situation of the black underclass is thus further reinforced by fear and anger on the grounds of race.

D. DISCUSSION QUESTIONS

1. How would you describe your social class or the social class of a close friend?

2. If sex and race are the first things Americans notice about strangers, at what stage in interaction do you think social class is noticed, and what are the **codes** for it?

3. Describe the social class structure of a racial group different from your own.

4. What conclusions can be drawn about the importance of race in determining social class in the United States?

5. Do you think that white racism varies according to social class in the United States, i.e., that blue-collar, middle- and upper-class whites typically have different forms of racism? Describe how.

E. RECOMMENDED READING

The classical sources in Western political theory for the ideas that some groups will liberate all are: (for the aristocracy) Plato, *The Republic,* and Aristotle, *Politics,* and *Nicomachean Ethics;* (for the middle class or bourgeoisie) John Locke, *Two Treatises of Government,* II, and Adam Smith, *The Wealth of Nations;* in interpretation of Locke, see C. B. MacPherson's *The Political Theory of Possessive Individualism,* and on natural law theory, see Edward Corwin, *The "Higher Law" Background of American Constitutional Law;* (for the working class) Karl Marx and Frederick Engels, "The Communist Manifesto," in Lawrence H. Simon, ed., *Karl Marx, Selected Writings;* for interpretations and further applications of Marx, see Nancy Holmstrom, "Race, Gender and Human Nature," in Naomi Zack, ed., *RACE/SEX,* and Sidney Hook, *From Hegel to Marx.* An activist application of Marxian ideology to undereducated workers is Paulo Freire's *Pedagogy of the Oppressed.* On the importance of race and class in childhood, see: C. E. Sleeter, ed., *Empowerment Through Multicultural Education;* Jennifer Clancy, "Multiracial Identity Assertion in the Sociopolitical Context of Primary Education," in Naomi Zack, ed., *American Mixed Race;* Helena Jia Hershel, "The Influence of Gender and Race Status on Self-Esteem During Childhood and Adolescence," in Naomi Zack, ed., *RACE/SEX.* On Native American rejection of Marxist ideology, see Ward Churchill, ed., *Marxism and Native Americans.*

On the historical study of childhood see: Philippe Ariès's analysis of ideas and practices of childhood in *Centuries of Childhood.* John Locke presents the modern model for middle-class child rearing in "Some Thoughts Concerning Education," in James A. Axtell, ed., *The Educational Writings of John Locke;* an interpretation of Locke's ideas is in Naomi Zack, *Bachelors of Science: Seventeenth Century Identity, Then and Now,* chapter 10. Nancy Chodorow in *The Reproduction of Mothering* explains how gender roles are reproduced in families. Cultural variations in forms of the family are discussed by Linda Nicholson in *Gender and History* and Naomi Zack in "'The Family' and Radical Family Theory," in Hilde Lindemann Nelson, ed., *Feminism and Families.*

On the effects of socioeconomic conditions on migrant childhood experience, see Robert Coles, *Uprooted Children.* See also Michelle Moody-Adams, "Race, Class and the Social Construction of Self-Respect," in John P. Pittman, ed., *African-American Perspectives and Philosophical Traditions.*

For socioeconomic statistics on American racial and ethnic groups see: *The Statistical Record of Black Americans; The Statistical Record of Asian Americans;*

The Statistical Record of Native North Americans, etc. Historical sources about free blacks during the period of slavery include: Ira Berlin, *Slaves Without Masters: The Free Negro in the Antebellum South;* David Cohen and Jack P. Greene, eds., *Neither Slave nor Free: The Freedmen of African Descent in the Slave Societies of the New World.* On differences in social class within the black group, see W. E. Cross, *Shades of Black: Diversity in African-American Identity.* For a study of how differences in social science research findings about blacks, vary with the race of the investigators, see Wade W. Nobles and Goddard L. Lawford, *Understanding the Black Family.*

For further reading on the intersection of race and social class, see: Robert and Jane Hollowell Coles, *Women of Crisis;* Angela Y. Davis, *Women, Race & Class;* Carl N. Degler, *Neither Black Nor White: Slavery and Race Relations in Brazil and the U.S.;* Gerald Horne, "On the Criminalization of a Race," in *Political Affairs;* Bill E. Lawson, ed., *The Underclass Question;* Thomas Sowell, *The Economics and Politics of Race: An International Perspective;* William Julius Wilson, *The Truly Disadvantaged.*

Y OU GO TO GROUP THERAPY ONCE A WEEK TO WORK ON A
VERY SPECIFIC PERSONAL PROBLEM THAT YOU SHARE WITH
OTHER MEMBERS OF THE GROUP. THE GROUP IS DIVERSE IN RACE,
ETHNICITY, GENDER, AND SEXUAL PREFERENCE, BUT IN OVER TWO
YEARS, NO ONE HAS EVER MENTIONED RACE. YOU THINK THAT THE
GROUP'S CONCERNS ARE DEEPER THAN RACE, BUT LATELY YOU'VE
NOTICED THAT PEOPLE SEEM TO GO OUT OF THEIR WAY TO AVOID
MENTIONING RACE. DO YOU THINK THE GROUP WOULD HAVE TO TALK
ABOUT RACE IN ORDER TO MAKE IMPORTANT PROGRESS ON THE
MAIN SUBJECT OF CONCERN, EVEN THOUGH THAT SUBJECT HAS
NOTHING TO DO WITH RACE?

CONCLUSION

INTRODUCTION

The chapter headings in this book by no means exhaust the topics under which race
has been studied and experienced in American life, or how we can think about it.
And if the reader has supplemented the text with more specific external readings, he
or she is aware of the ways in which the ideas presented here have been general and
inconclusive. This is partly due to the *toolbox* intention behind the book: Tools for
thinking about race do not determine what you will think about, or your conclusions.
Also, race itself, as an idea or complex of ideas, is general and inconclusive. Therefore, to bring some closure to the discussions begun here, it might be helpful to consider two things: (A) Racial thinking in real life requires an awareness of boundaries;
and (B) Americans might be ready for a new paradigm of race.

A. BOUNDARIES AND RACE

The notion of **boundaries,** and drawing and respecting boundaries, can be borrowed
from contemporary clinical and self-help psychology. When a person, P, sets boundaries in an interaction with another person, Q, P communicates to Q that certain areas
of $P's$ life, person, and experience are "off-limits" to Q. This usually means that in
order to remain in $P's$ good graces, Q must refrain from evaluating, attempting to
control, taking possession of, or even acquiring information about whatever is on $P's$
side of the boundary. This concept of boundaries involves an assumption that no two

people can or should be all things to one another, that different degrees of intimacy are appropriate in different relationships, that people will respect the needs of other people to maintain different kinds of distance from them, and that everyone lives his or her own life.

People have strong emotional responses in matters of race, not due to arbitrary whim or temperament, but because they have directly learned, been taught, or made generalizations resulting in, important factual and moral beliefs. The varied ways in which beliefs about race are connected to emotions is in itself reason to approach racial matters with respect for the boundaries of others, and to let it be known what one's own boundaries are. This is not to say that racial issues ought not to be rationally discussed, criticized, and negotiated whenever problems arise. But it is to say that boundaries need to be respected in such discussions so that everyone has the space to take responsibility for what he or she brings to the discussion. We need to assume that our interlocutors are capable of the same reflection and careful thought that we are.

If it seems paradoxical to speak of boundaries in the context of a discussion about race in a society that, as noted in this book's Introduction, is divided, or splintered, by race, we need to remember some basics about human rights. Many human rights are negative. ***Negative rights*** are the freedom to do what the law does not prohibit, without interference. The worst violations of human rights that have been committed on the grounds of race, such as assault, mutilation, murder, theft, degradation, and persecution, have involved transgressions of the boundaries of others in ways that impact on survival. Boundaries are not necessarily limitations on where people may go physically, but on what they may do in the range of actions that affect the rights of others. In this sense, forced segregation by race is a violation of the boundaries of those segregated because it limits their freedom of action. Voluntary segregation by race may be either an exercise of boundary rights, or an expression of other racial problems, or both.

A respect for boundaries in the relatively gentle arenas of public discussion, identity, and individual life choices ought to be easier to secure than were the fundamental rights to life and liberty that are the foundation for setting boundaries. The right to freedom of speech includes a right to try to change the mind of another. However, one does not have a right to change someone's mind if that person does not want to engage in discussion or refuses to discuss the topic in question. And one does not have a right to impose moral judgments about what other people ought to think and do, so long as their thoughts and actions do not harm others.

In American society, freedom includes individual ***autonomy,*** which literally means "self-rule." Individuals develop their capacity to make decisions and they have the power to act on their decisions. Racial identity, however, is connected with membership in groups and loyalties to the decisions made by other group members and leaders. Therefore, racial autonomy has traditionally meant the self-rule of groups rather than individuals. The combination of individual and group autonomy may require individuals to draw boundaries within racial groups.

Finally, boundaries concern what people do, their spheres of free decision and action, rather than what they are, or their identities. In order to define and protect their identities, people draw ***borders.*** On a biological level, individuals must maintain borders between themselves and the external environment in order to survive. On a social level, in which some identities are important for status and success, the need for borders may result in aversion to those who represent low status and failure. For example, those who are white, young, or male may have social borders between themselves and those who are nonwhite, old, or female. But those who are nonwhite, old, or female may also have borders of their own to protect their identities.

B. A NEW PARADIGM OF RACE?

A *cultural paradigm* is a set of assumptions about an area of human life, or the world, that is shared by a sufficiently influential number of people so that the set of assumptions is part of common sense. The paradigm functions as a theory that explains past and present experiences, and it generates predictions and expectations about future experience.

The current paradigm of race divides people into races as a matter of biological fact, and it attaches different expectations regarding culture and behavior to those racial groups. A new paradigm of race might begin with knowledge that there is no biological foundation for the different racial groups. As a result, what was previously thought of as race might now be thought of as ethnicity. Since ethnicity is now accepted as a fluid, changeable, interlocking system of human categories and lifestyle choices, racial identity and racial membership could as well be viewed as a fluid, changeable, interlocking system of human categories and lifestyle choices. Mixed-race realities support this reconfiguration of race as ethnicity, and so does consideration of the ways in which ideas of race have changed over time and across cultures.

When people attach strong differences to what they think of as racial difference, these attachments could be viewed as beliefs that they are entitled to, much as they are entitled to varied religious beliefs. When the practice of these beliefs is a source of fulfillment and self-expression, they would merit the same respect as the practice of other beliefs that derive from cultural traditions. When the beliefs about racial difference result in harm to other human beings, they would be viewed as moral defects, or sadistic and criminal delusions, and treated accordingly; when such beliefs are self-destructive, they would require both psychological and social treatment.

A new paradigm of race might have some detachment from race built into it that would allow for the possibility that racial categorization, identity, and struggle will pass out of history. From this detached perspective, race would be no more than an idea about human beings that was useful for organizing society in the past, but is increasingly without use or benefit as time goes on.

C. DISCUSSION QUESTIONS

1. Suppose that students who belong to racial minorities sit together in a classroom that is predominantly white. What kinds of boundaries or borders might they be drawing?

2. Name some acceptable boundaries and borders concerning race that in your opinion are worthy of respect. Name some that are not worthy of respect.

3. Do you think Americans are ready for a new paradigm of race? How do you think such a paradigm might be different from the old paradigm?

4. If people who are attached to the present paradigm are offended by the new paradigm, what rights do they have in the matter?

D. RECOMMENDED READING

For ideas about boundaries as applicable to race, see the following: Laurence Thomas, "Moral Deference," in John P. Pittman, ed., *African-American Perspectives and Philosophical Traditions;* Audre Lorde, "The Uses of Anger: Women Responding to Racism," in Anne Minas, ed., *Gender Basics;* Glenn Loury, "Self-Censorship in Public Discourse," in Glenn Loury, ed., *One By One From the Inside Out.* On borders and aversion, see Iris Marion Young, *Justice and the Politics of Difference,* chapter 5. For a psychological analysis of boundaries presented in terms of "image management," see Irving Goffman, *The Presentation of Self in Everyday Life.* A comprehensive philosophical discussion of rights is Judith Jarvis Thomson's *The Realm of Rights.* The classic liberal source for freedom of thought, speech, and lifestyle is John Stuart Mill's essay *On Liberty.*

The canonical source for the current concept of a paradigm is Thomas S. Kuhn, *The Structure of Scientific Revolutions.* Laurie Shrage presents a playful view of racial identity as changing choices, in "Passing Beyond the Other Race or Sex," in Naomi Zack, ed., *RACE/SEX.*

GLOSSARY

Note: Words are defined as they are used in the context of this book and related sources.

abstract   Pertaining to parts of things that are identified as members of a group; the process of identifying those parts.

affirm   To recognize in a positive or benevolent way.

affirmative action   Strategy of increasing educational and employment opportunities for disadvantaged groups, especially women and members of racial minorities, by requiring their admission to situations where they were previously excluded or are not present in numbers proportional to their presence in a wider population.

African American   American of African descent; black.

ambiguous   Unable to be determined. A sexually ambiguous person is someone who does not appear to be definitely male or female.

American Jewish identity   The meaning of being Jewish to Jews who are Americans.

anachronism   An opinion, belief, or action that would be more characteristic of a different time in history than the one in which it occurs or to which it is applied.

analyze   To break down into the simplest conceptual parts.

androgynous   Having neither male nor female sexual traits; appearing to have neither male nor female sexual traits.

appropriation   Takeover of something without the right to do so.

aracial   Without any racial identity; without specific racial identity.

archetype   A generalized image of a kind or type of person, which is shared within a culture.

Asian   Racial designation for descendants of people originating in areas west of the Pacific Ocean and east of the Caspian Sea.

assimilation   Process of becoming part of a dominant culture by taking on its most important characteristics in place of one's own subordinate group characteristics.

atheist   Person who does not believe in God on the grounds that God does not exist.

authentic appearance   Looking and behaving as members of one's racial or ethnic group are expected to appear and behave.

authentic provenance   Having and being known to have the ancestry of the group that one belongs to.

authentic solidarity   Loyalty and helpfulness to members of one's racial or ethnic group, simply because they are members of one's own group.

authenticity   Genuineness or realness as the member of a racial or ethnic group.

authority   Recognized power that is vested in an individual, group or organization.

autonomy   Individual self-rule; the freedom of individuals to choose their actions and develop as persons.

aversive   Avoiding; disliking; rejecting.

basic rules of logic   The assumptions behind systematic thought, such as the rule of noncontradiction: a statement cannot be both true and false at the same time.

berdache   Social role characteristics of people in non-Western cultures, who are accepted as members of the opposite sex, within their communities.

bigotry   Devotion to one's own beliefs or group to the point of intolerance of difference, or hatred of others.

biologism   Belief that important social aspects of human life and behavior can be explained by the science of biology.

biracial   Descended from two races.

black   Appearing to belong to the Negro race or having an ancestor of Negro descent; Black (with capital *B*) usually refers to the ethnicity of black people.

Black Power   The ability of black people to affirm and liberate themselves, an idea and term formulated during activist movements in the 1960s and 1970s.

black underclass   Poor, usually urban, inadequately educated part of black population with high rates of unemployment and involvement in the criminal justice system as defendants.

blood quantum   Percentage of Native American ancestry required for recognized membership in some tribes or for designation as Indian by the U.S. federal government.

borders   Ways of preserving personal identity or what an individual believes the self to be.

boundaries   The limits an individual wants to set on the behavior of others with regard to that individual, usually within the fundamental rights and liberties of that individual.

bourgeoisie   Middle class; property-owners or owners of means of production in society.

breed   In biological terms, a type within a species, having common inherited traits that are usually visible.

breeding   In social class terms, a combination of preferred or believed to be superior ancestry and upbringing.

capitalism   Competitive economic system of private ownership of property and the means of production where goods are produced for motives of monetary profit and workers are employed for wages or salaries.

Chicano/a   Preferred term for Mexican Americans.

citizenship rights   The entitlements of individuals who are recognized by the government to be fully participating members of a political body, such as the right to vote and the right to full protection under the laws.

civil rights   Basic freedom and entitlements of citizenship of members of a society that others may not violate without legal punishment.

Civil Rights Movement   Social activism that resulted in racial integration and voting rights for black Americans by the mid-1960s.

class theory   Set of hypotheses about groups in society that explain how they have developed and now interact as social classes.

classic racism   Dislike or hatred of members of other racial groups, usually nonwhites, often with intention to harm them.

client   Recipient of a social service.

code   When one thing is a sign for another, sometimes used as a verb, e.g., her clothes *code* black.

cognitive   Pertaining to intellectual processes and activities, in contrast to emotional ones, for example.

collateral kin   Relative(s) having common ancestor(s) but not common parents, e.g., cousins.

collective responsibility   When all members of a group, individually or as a group, are responsible for the actions of some members.

color-blind   Lacking in discrimination when race is assumed to be mainly a matter of skin color.

colored   Term for Negro in the United States before 1960s, now considered racist; term for mixed race in South Africa.

colorism   Social and personal ranking of people based on skin hue, especially within a nonwhite racial group, with lighter hues preferred.

communism Economic and political system in which major means of production are owned by the government in the name of the people.

compensation Benefit conferred on account of harm suffered or disadvantage experienced, to give recipient(s) better opportunities to succeed in life.

concept The meaning of a word.

concrete egalitarianism Position that people of all races and ethnicities are equal as members of their distinct groups, not as individuals.

consensus Broad agreement on an issue or sameness in opinion or belief, often developed through open discussion.

consequentialism Moral theory in which the goodness or badness of actions is assessed according to their consequences.

conservatism Set of beliefs and practices that in cultural and political contexts imply a resistance to change.

covert racism Hidden racism, often deliberately concealed.

creed System of beliefs that people are born into or choose; to say that something is a matter of creed avoids pronouncing on its truth or falsity.

criteria Requirements, conditions, or standards that have to be met before something can be granted; characteristics or traits that have to be present for something to be judged to be of a certain kind or type.

critical race theory Analysis of the role of the U.S. legal system and capitalist economy in maintaining injustice based on race, may be developed through narratives from personal experience.

critical theory Analysis of the power relations and dominant-subordinate behavior in a society, which are unjust and not always recognized for what they are by participants.

cultural authenticity Displaying knowledge of the history and tradition of one's racial or ethnic group, which display is expected by others.

cultural paradigm A set of beliefs about a certain area of human life, or the world, that are widely shared within a culture. Experience is described and explained in terms of the paradigm and predictions and expectations are based on it.

cultural genocide The deliberate destruction of a group's cultural practices so that they die out as a tradition that can be taught to succeeding generations.

customary That which is normal or usual, frequently done, observed, believed, etc.

de facto In existence or in fact; term used to refer to segregation that is not legislated.

de jure By law; term used to refer to legalized segregation.

descriptive The non-evaluative nature of a verbal account that is meant to relate how things are in fact.

diaspora All the members of a racial or ethnic group in different geographical locations when, due to historical circumstances, they are not presently located in the same geographical area.

discrimination Actions or choices in favor of members of one group as opposed to another, based on their racial or ethnic classification.

diversity Noticeable difference(s) in gender, race, or ethnicity that have consequences in society; the presence together of people with such difference.

Ebonics Variation of English used by American ethnic blacks, composed of traditional black cultural speech and current slang.

egalitarianism Position that all human beings are equal, as individuals, regardless of race or ethnicity.

eliminative That which does away with a concept or idea in use because it is self-contradictory or has no factual basis.

elitism Affirmation of the privileged position of a social group with natural or cultural advantages.

emancipation Freedom, usually following a situation of oppression.

emancipatory tradition   Intellectual and political practices that are intended to further or result in emancipation for a particular group.

empiricism   Commitment that statements about reality be based on observation and investigation.

entitlements   Special rights to social or material goods that are conferred on some groups.

environmental racism   Harm or destruction of environment that effects people unequally as racial groups.

ethical   Pertaining to right and wrong; a person who does the right thing is an ethical person.

ethnically neutral   Having no preferences pertaining to the ethnicity of others, or having no evident ethnic identity oneself.

ethnicity   Human cultural traits as learned behavior; the combination of learned cultural behavior with a specific ancestry and physical appearance.

feminism   Contemporary interdisciplinary scholarly thought, personal ideology, and social and political activism that affirms the rights and value of women and analyzes the contemporary and historical conditions of their exclusion and oppression.

fighting words   Words that directly incite others to violent action.

folk   People that share beliefs in a culture; the lay public or mass of citizens, rather than educated elites or public officials.

folk model   Description of ideas or behavior that laypeople share within a culture.

fractional   Divided into numbers of less than one, as in a type of mixed-race identity that specifies the different parts of racial ancestry in numerical fractions.

freedmen   Former African American slaves who were freed.

full blood   A monoracial person, usually also displaying common notions of racial or ethnic authenticity; used especially in context of Native American identity.

fundamentalists   In a religious sense, people who believe in the literal truth of their religion as set down in a holy book.

gender   The behavioral and social role aspects of maleness or femaleness.

general   Pertaining to a large number or all of the individual things or people in a group, as wholes.

generic   Unspecified, as in *generic mixed-race identity.*

genocide   Deliberate destruction of an entire group of people or their culture.

good evidence   Factual reports that have been verified and are sufficient to support a claim, generalization, or conclusion.

grand theory   System of explanation and prediction that applies to all the subjects in an area of inquiry.

Harlem Renaissance   Period during the 1920s and 1930s when black arts and literature began to flourish on the basis of the pride of American blacks in their achievements and culture.

hate speech   Offensive speech that is intended to insult and harm others on account of their race, ethnicity or gender.

Hispanic   An ethnic designation referring to a Spanish surname, descent from Spanish-speaking people, or residents of Portugal or Latin America, includes Latinos[/as] and Chicanos[as], although some members of the latter two groups have rejected Hispanic designation because they have no Spanish ancestry.

homogeneous   The same within, having similar members.

homophobic   Fearing and/or hating homosexuals and lesbians.

hyperdescent   System in which children of mixed parentage acquire the social and racial status of the parent whose social and racial status is higher.

hypodescent   System in which children of mixed parentage acquire the social and racial status of the parent whose social and racial status is lower.

identification   Categorization of a person by others in terms of race, ethnicity, or gender. (More broadly, other categories also apply, such as age and physical ableness.)

identify   To categorize another by race or ethnicity; to put oneself in the place of another or imagine oneself to be another specific individual or member of a racial or ethnic group different from one's own; to state one's race or ethnicity.

identity   Self-categorization of a person in terms of race, ethnicity, or gender (more broadly, other categories also apply, such as occupation); in the philosophical sense, that which makes a person the same person throughout changes; also, what a person is to himself or herself.

identity politics   Formal or informal political system in which people vote or otherwise exert influence as members of racial, gendered, ethnic, or other groups with interests and status unrecognized by the majority (for instance, homosexuals, lesbians, and the disabled).

ideology   System of beliefs about how the world ought to be, based on moral assumptions, economic interests, value judgments, or fundamental political beliefs.

inclusive   Capable of containing whole units instead of an addition of fractions to make one whole, as in *inclusive mixed-race identity* that encompasses all different aspects of a person's racial ancestry.

indigenism   Political and ideological liberation theory of contemporary Native Americans based on their ancestors being the original, or "native" inhabitants of North and South America.

institutionalized   Being part of an institution so that one's life is lived according to its rules, applies, e.g., to prison inmates, lifelong social service clients.

institutional racism   Formal practices and traditions in social organizations, or customs, that harm some racial groups or deny them the same opportunities as other racial groups.

integration   Freedom of physical movement for people of nonwhite races that results in their presence among whites in political, economic, educational, and social life.

intellectual error   Mistake in opinion due to error in reasoning, ignorance, or incorrect judgment of evidence.

intellectual remedy   Correction of intellectual error by providing information or pointing out error in reasoning or judging evidence.

intent of the law   What the law is supposed to accomplish in its application.

intersection   When two or more categories in which a person is classified and identified work in combination to create a category or form of experience different from that of any of the categories originally combined.

intersexed   Having the primary biological traits of both males and females, or having neither.

justice   Fairness in civic and political life; characteristic of laws and legal practices that are in agreement with broad moral or ethical intuitions.

la raza   Concept and reality of people of Latin American countries as one race containing racial variation within itself.

Latino[/a]   The ethnic category of people descended from residents of Latin America.

leisure   Conditions necessary for recreation and self-care and development.

lesbian   A woman who prefers other women as sexual partners, or in feminist contexts, the centering of women's experience.

liberation   Freedom after oppression; actions undertaken to achieve freedom; the goal of freedom for an oppressed group.

liberation theory   Hypothesis, plan, description, ideology, or analysis of current cultural conditions that is intended to achieve freedom for a particular group(s).

line   Relations connecting direct ancestors or direct descendents; pre-eighteenth century concept of race.

logic   Formal system of rules of thought.

logical contradictories   Two statements that cannot both be true and cannot both be false, e.g., "No S is P" and "Some S is P."

mainstream   Dominant part of American society including the upper class, professionals, and all those active in civic, social, corporate, educational, and political life; "the system."

marginalize   Keep outside the center or exclude from full participation and empowerment.

Marxist ideology   Marxism; ideology based on the writings of Karl Marx and Frederick Engels.

matriarchal   Ruled by women.

melting pot   Model of the United States as a place in which individuals from different cultures would contribute to one new culture through work, civic life, and social life, and would lose their original ethnicities through intermarriage and assimilation.

meritocracy   System in which individuals are rewarded on the basis of their demonstrated aptitudes, skills, and achievements.

microdiversity   Racial diversity on an individual level, as is present in individuals of mixed racial ancestry.

minstrelsy   Late nineteenth- and early twentieth-century theatrical genre in which white men wore "blackface" to imitate both black men and women in stereotypical roles.

miscegenation   Racial mixture in human reproduction.

mixed race   Having ancestry of more than one race.

monoethnic   Having ancestry of all one ethnicity.

monoracial   Having ancestry of all one race.

moral   Ethical; having to do with right or wrong, usually in instances involving important harm or benefit to people.

moral status   Standing of a person as a moral agent and as someone who is the object of moral or immoral behavior by others.

mulatto   Person with one black and one white parent; after 1920, term came to mean a person with any degree of mixed black and white ancestry.

mulatto elite   Before 1920, part of black population that was mixed race and had advantages of interactions with whites as well as middle-class education, employment, cultural experience.

multiculturalism   Program that includes people from different cultures as well as their distinctive intellectual, literary, and artistic products.

multiethnic   Having ancestry from two or more ethnic groups.

multiracial   Having ancestry from more than two different races; sometimes used as a synonym for *mixed race* to include biracial.

myth   Shared beliefs about events or people that serve a social purpose but have little or no basis in reality.

narrative   An account of experiences and events that focuses on the particulars of what takes place, rather than a generalization about types of experiences or events; a story.

Native American   Member of the group of descendants of people who inhabited the Americas before European colonialism, or a member of a group that identifies with such descendants.

nativism   Late nineteenth and early twentieth century belief that Americans born in the U.S. were culturally and morally superior to immigrants.

natural aristocracy   Group of people believed to be superior to others solely due to traits they are born with (not originally a racial concept).

natural law   Laws believed to be given to men by God, believed by Christians to be a foundation for democratic constitutional government with safeguards for individual rights, especially the right to own private property.

naturalness   Quality of being present by nature or in nature, without human intervention or cultural influence.

negative right   A right not to have certain actions taken with regard to one, for instance, the right to be left alone so long as one is obeying the laws.

neoconservative   Since 1970, characteristic of political programs and individuals who reject extreme social changes, support American capitalism, and favor minimal government spending and intervention in the lives of private citizens.

non-ethnic   Having no evident ethnic identity.

nonmaterialistic   Not primarily concerned with physical objects of monetary value or with money.

nonobservant   Characteristic of some Jews whereby they do not follow the religious practices of Judaism.

normative   The nature of a proposal or persuasive account of how things ought to be, based on assumptions about values and moral goodness.

octoroon   Person who has seven white great-grandparents and one black great-grandparent.

offensive   Shocking; disgusting; emotionally or morally upsetting.

one-drop rule   American social and legal custom of classifying anyone with one black ancestor, regardless of how far back, as black.

"other"   Category to be checked on official forms when the standard racial alternatives of black, white, Asian, or Indian are not checked.

outcome   Numbers of women and members of racial minority group who gain access in a hiring, admissions, or promotion process.

overgeneralization   A conclusion or generalization based on insufficient evidence or experience.

overt racism   Racism that is deliberate and explicit.

paradigm   Set of shared beliefs through which an area of reality is interpreted.

parameters   Conceptual boundaries, foundations, or restrictions.

pass   To present oneself as different from what one is, especially used in reference to people with black ancestry who present themselves as white.

patriarchy   Social system in which men dominate in all important areas of life, usually associated with their roles as fathers and husbands but extending to public life as well.

person   A being with legal rights and recognized social and moral importance.

personal authenticity   Courage to express one's beliefs and opinions or display how one is, when others disagree or disapprove.

personal identity   Philosophical concept of the sameness of persons which is usually determined by what cannot be changed if the person is to be judged the same person; how a person seems to be to his or her self.

perspective   Point of view or position from which one understands and interprets areas of knowledge and reality.

pluralism   Combination of distinct ethnic and/or racial groups in public life.

pluralistic society   A public whole composed of different racial or ethnic groups that are treated equally and valued by their members and members of other groups for their distinct identities.

population(s)   Current scientific concept of a group of people who share some of the physical similarities that previously were attributed to race.

positive right   An entitlement to something fundamental to citizenship, for example, the right to vote.

pragmatic   Practical, a form of calculation or evaluation that places a strong emphasis on results, consequences, and material benefits.

preferential treatment   Form of affirmative action in which qualified women or nonwhites are preferred over white males to whom they are equal in qualifications.

principles   Rules for behavior, especially moral rules.

profit   In production, the monetary difference between the material, labor and capital costs of production and the price received for the products.

proletariat   Marxist term for nineteenth- and twentieth-century laborers; generally, the working class.

proving a negative   Convincing or persuading others that something is not the case or does not exist. Usually the burden of proof is on the person who asserts that something *is* the case or that something *does* exist.

psychologies of race   The ways in which beliefs about race motivate people on individual levels.

public policy   Set of rules for official action, intended to bring about an end desired by citizens or mandated by law.

quadroon   Person who has three white grandparents and one black grandparent.

quotas   In affirmative action contexts, specific numbers of members of racial minorities, or women, that are required to be hired or admitted even if their qualifications do not fully merit it.

race   Idea of a distinct biological type of human being; term referring generally to racial difference and racial relations.

racial determinism   Belief that racial membership alone causes other, nonracial human characteristics.

racial essences   Idea of important general traits that all members of a distinct race are assumed to share, causing them to be members of that race, now recognized not to have a scientific basis.

racialist   Person who believes in the existence of races as a biological reality.

racism   Beliefs and practices that harm members of some races and not others.

racist   Racialist who harbors ill will or intent to do harm against others due to their racial membership; adjective describing the beliefs or actions of racists.

rationalize   Give reasons for something that justify it, which are not the real reasons or motives.

received opinion   Belief(s) widely accepted and not normally questioned.

reconfigure   To change the way in which something is defined without changing it completely; to shift a perspective on an area of human experience.

reduces   Translates into something else that is conceptually more precise.

reparation   Compensation that includes recognition that harm has been injustly inflicted.

reproduction   Continual creation of social structures, as well as oppressive categories, within a culture; biological production of next generation.

reverse discrimination   When a group that previously practiced discrimination becomes the object of discrimination.

rhizomatic   Pertaining to the horizontal root structure of plants that grow along the ground and do not have main taproots; used as a metaphor for mixed-race identity that can spring up in one generation.

role-model argument   Argument in favor of affirmative action on the basis of its putting members from previously excluded groups in new social and professional roles.

rooted   Deriving nourishment from soil through roots, especially a main taproot; used as a metaphor for monoracial identity traced back in time through ancestry.

segregation   Policy of keeping people physically separate in employment, education, housing, social activities, etc., on the basis of race, especially when nonwhite racial membership results in exclusion from goods of society monopolized by the white majority.

Semite   Member of a Caucasian race that now consists of Jews and Arabs.

separatism   Movement or belief that members of a distinct racial, ethnic, or gender group ought to withdraw from other groups in society, socially, economically, politically, and geographically (if possible).

sex   Biological difference based on reproductive function and chromosomal markers.

sex drive   A strong desire to engage in sexual activity, assumed to be universally present in human beings.

sexual dymorphism Conceptual system that posits the existence of two biological sexes, male and female.

sexual objects Persons or things who, without regard for their own feelings, are sexually sought after by others.

sexual subjects Persons who actively desire others, usually with the power to actualize their desires.

social caste Inherited social class.

social class Group in society that has a distinctive status and experience, economically, politically and socially; according to Marxism, the social class of a group is determined by its relationship to the most important means of production.

social entity A group of people that interact with one another based on a shared perception of their membership in that group.

social group A number of people identified as a collectivity, may or may not be a social entity.

social reality The beliefs and practices that individuals have to take into account in interacting with others; the things that most members of a society believe exist.

socially constructed Not present in nature but created and maintained in culture and often thought to be "natural."

socially intelligible Clear or understandable to others in the same society.

stereotype Fixed, often derogatory, idea about members of a group that is applied to all members, regardless of individual difference; may be true of some members of the group or of no members of the group.

stigma A mark or sign of something undesirable.

strategy A type of action that is a means to an end.

suffragettes Late nineteenth- and early twentieth-century women activists who organized, wrote, spoke, and demonstrated to secure the right of women to vote.

tactics Goal directed actions, usually more specific than strategy.

taxonomy System of types or categories in an area of knowledge or reality.

thinking critically Looking at the problems or falseness in a belief or opinion; investigating the basis of beliefs and analyzing them; following rules of logic and good evidence; thinking for oneself as opposed to accepting beliefs and opinions of others.

token An individual who is meant to represent his or her entire race.

traditional Pertaining to how things were done in the past.

traditional nonwhite identities Identities that conform to official categories of black, Asian, and Indian.

traditional values Aspects of social and private life that are sought after or retained because they are thought to be morally good and based on past custom.

transsexual The gender characteristics of an individual whose gender does not match the biological sex he or she was characterized by at birth, (also used as a noun).

trope A part of something that symbolizes the whole of it.

unintentional racism Speech or action that harms members of some racial group(s), though not done for that reason.

universalism Position that all human beings are or should be the same in certain ways, regardless of race, ethnicity, nationality, gender or any other form of difference.

utility Something that is of benefit to human beings.

valorize Honor, idealize.

WASP Anachronym for White Anglo-Saxon Protestant.

white Racial designation referring to European ancestry and appearance, or more formally, the absence of nonwhite ancestry.

white purity White racial identity that rests on both the absence of and aversion to nonwhites.

white race treason   Repudiation of the privileges of whiteness by white people who think that these privileges are morally unjustified and racist against nonwhites.

white supremacy   Belief that whites are superior to nonwhites in important human traits and that they ought to dominate nonwhites in society.

white trash   Derogatory popular name for the white group that is poor and/or culturally backward, now sometimes used affirmatively.

whiteness studies   Scholarly writings about the cultural aspects of white racial identity and identification.

womanism   Contemporary form of feminism developed by black women writers and scholars that emphasizes their experience and knowledge, as well as their sources of spiritual inspiration in religion and the lives of other black women.

women's liberation   Term for the movement and ideology of women's emancipation, or for feminism, that was in use during the 1960s and 1970s.

word   Sound or mark that symbolizes something other than itself.

Yiddish   High German dialect written in Hebrew letters, used by European Jews.

Zionism   Jewish religious and political beliefs and actions that hold Israel, as the original Jewish homeland, to be of central importance to Jews throughout the Jewish diaspora.

BIBLIOGRAPHY

Note: Complete citations of anthologies are listed under editors' last names when the anthologies are listed more than once.

Alcoff, Linda. "Mestizo Identity." In *American Mixed Race,* ed. Naomi Zack, 257–278.

Allen, Anita L. "The Role Model Argument and Faculty Diversity." In *African-American Perspectives and Philosophical Traditions,* ed. John P. Pittman, 267–281.

Allen, James Paul, and Eugene James Turner. *We The People: An Atlas of America's Ethnic Diversity.* New York: Macmillan, 1988.

Allen, Paula Gunn. *The Sacred Hoop: Recovering the Feminine in American Indian Traditions.* Boston: Beacon Press, 1986.

Allison, Dorothy. *Bastard Out of Carolina.* New York: Dutton, 1992.

Alvarez, Julia. *How the Garcia Girls Lost Their Accents.* Chapel Hill, NC: Algonquin Books, 1991.

Alonso, William, and Paul Starr, eds. *The Politics of Numbers.* New York: Russell Sage Foundation, 1987.

Anderson, Benedict. *Imagined Communities.* London: Verso Books, 1983.

Anzuldúa, Gloria. *Borderlands/La Frontera: The New Mestiza.* San Francisco: Sisters/Aunt Lute Book Company, 1987.

———. *Making Face, Making Soul.* San Francisco: Aunt Lute, 1990.

Appiah, Anthony. "Racisms." In *Anatomy of Racism,* ed. David Theo Goldberg, 3–17.

———. *In My Father's House.* Oxford: Oxford University Press, 1992.

———. " 'But Would that Still be Me?': Notes on Gender, 'Race' Ethnicity as Sources of Identity." In *RACE/SEX,* ed. Naomi Zack, 75–82.

Appiah, K. Anthony. "Race, Culture, Identity." In *Color Consciousness: The Political Morality of Race,* ed. K. Anthony Appiah and Amy Gutman, 3–75. Princeton, NJ: Princeton University Press, 1996.

Ariés, Philippe. *Centuries of Childhood.* Trans. Robert Baldick, New York: Alfred A. Knopf, 1962.

Aristotle. *The Politics.* Trans. T. A. Sinclair, ed. Trevor J. Saunders. New York: Penguin, 1981.

———. *Nicomachean Ethics.* Trans. Terence Irwin. Indianapolis: Hackett, 1985.

Augenbraum, Harold, and Ilan Stavans, eds. *Growing Up Latino.* Boston: Houghton Mifflin Company, 1993.

Azoulay, Karya Gibel. *Black, Jewish, and Interracial.* Durham, NC: Duke University Press, 1997.

Bell, Derrick. *And We Are Not Saved: The Elusive Quest for Racial Justice.* New York: Basic Books, 1987.

Bell, Linda, and David Blumenfeld, eds. *Overcoming Sexism and Racism.* Lanham, MD: Rowman and Littlefield, 1994.

Belliotti, Raymond A. *Seeking Identity.* Lawrence, KS: University Press of Kansas, 1995.

Berlin, Ira. *Slaves Without Masters: The Free Negro in the Antebellum South.* New York: Pantheon Books, 1975.

Bernal, Martin. *Black Athena: Vol. I, The Fabrication of Ancient Greece, 1785–1985.* New Brunswick, NJ: Rutgers University Press, 1987.

Berry, Bernita C. "'I Just See People': Exercises in Learning the Effects of Racism and Sexism." In *Overcoming Sexism and Racism,* ed. Linda Bell and David Blumenfeld, 45–51.

Bhabha, Homi. *The Location of Culture.* New York: Routledge, 1994.

Boxill, Bernard. "The Morality of Reparation." *Social Theory and Practice* 2, no. 1 (1972): 113–122.

Bradford, Judith, and Crispin Sartwell. "Voiced Bodies/Embodied Voices." In *RACE/SEX,* ed. Naomi Zack, 191–204.

Bradshaw, C. K. "Beauty and the Beast: On Racial Ambiguity." In *Racially Mixed People in America,* ed. Maria P. P. Root, 77–89.

Brown, L. S., and M. P. P. Root, eds. *Diversity and Complexity in Feminist Therapy.* New York: Haworth Press, 1990.

Butler, Judith. *Gender Trouble: Feminism and the Subversion of Identity.* New York: Routledge, 1990.

Butler, Robert Olen. *A Good Scent from a Strange Mountain: Stories.* New York: H. Holt, 1992.

Callicott, Baird J. *In Defense of the Land Ethic.* Albany: State University of New York Press, 1989.

Card, Claudia. "Race, Racism, and Ethnicity." In *Overcoming Sexism and Racism,* eds. Linda Bell and David Blumenfeld, 141–152.

Chavez, Linda. *Out of the Barrio: Toward a New Politics of Hispanic Assimilation.* New York: Basic Books, 1991.

Chin, Curtis. *Witness Aloud: Lesbian, Gay and Bisexual Asian/Pacific American Writing.* New York: Asian American Writers' Workshop, 1993.

Chodorow, Nancy. *The Reproduction of Mothering.* Berkeley: University of California Press, 1978.

Churchill, Ward. *Fantasies of the Master Race,* ed. M. Annette Jaimes. Monroe, ME: Common Courage Press, 1992.

———. *Struggle for the Land.* Monroe, ME: Common Courage Press, 1992.

———. *Indians Are Us?* Monroe, ME: Common Courage Press, 1994.

———, ed. *From a Native Son: Selected Essays on Indigenism, 1985–1995.* Boston: South End Press, 1996.

———, ed. *Marxism and Native Americans.* Boston: South End Press, 1993.

Clancy, Jennifer. "Multiracial Identity Assertion in the Sociopolitical Context of Primary Education." In *American Mixed Race,* ed. Naomi Zack, 211–220.

Clements, Susan. "Five Arrows." In *American Mixed Race,* ed. Naomi Zack, 3–12.

Cohen, David W., and Jack P. Greene, eds. *Neither Slave nor Free: The Freedmen of African Descent in the Slave Societies of the New World.* Baltimore: Johns Hopkins University Press, 1972.

Coles, Robert. *Uprooted Children.* Pittsburgh: University of Pittsburgh Press, 1970.

Coles, Robert, and Jane Hollowell Coles. *Women of Crisis.* New York: Delacorte Press/ Seymour Lawrence, 1978.

Collins, Patricia Hill. *Black Feminist Thought.* London: Harper Collins Academic Press, 1990.

———. "Learning to Think for Ourselves: Malcolm X's Black Nationalism Reconsidered." In *Malcolm X: In Our Own Image,* ed. Joe Wood, 75–87. New York: Doubleday, 1992.

Copi, Irving M. *Introduction to Logic.* New York: Macmillan, 1961.

Corlett, Angelo J. "Parallels of Ethnicity and Gender." In *RACE/SEX,* ed. Naomi Zack, 83–94.

Corwin, Edward S. *The "Higher Law" Background of American Constitutional Law.* Ithaca, NY, and London: Cornell University Press, 1986.

Cox, Oliver C. *Caste, Class and Race.* New York: Doubleday, 1948.

Crenshaw, Kimberly. "Demarginalizing the Intersection of Race and Sex: A Black Feminist Critique of Antidiscrimination Doctrine, Feminist Theory, and Antiracist Politics." In *Living With Contradictions,* ed. Alison Jagger, 39–52.

Cross, W. E. *Shades of Black: Diversity in African-American Identity.* Philadelphia: Temple University Press, 1991.

Davis, Angela Y. *Women, Race & Class.* New York: Random House, 1983.

Davis, F. James. *Who is Black?* University Park, PA: Pennsylvania State University Press, 1991.

———. "The Hawaiian Alternative to the One-Drop Rule." In *American Mixed Race,* ed. Naomi Zack, 115–132.

Davis, Marilyn P. *Mexican Voices/American Dreams.* New York: Henry Holt and Company, 1990.

Davy, Kate. "Outing Whiteness: A Feminist/Lesbian Project." *Theatre Journal* 47, no. 2 (May 1995): 189–205.

Day, Beth. *Sexual Life Between Blacks and Whites: The Roots of Racism.* New York: World Publishing, Times Mirror, 1972.

Degler, Carl N. *Neither Black Nor White: Slavery and Race Relations in Brazil and the U.S.* New York: Macmillan, 1971.

Delgado, Richard. *Critical Race Theory: The Cutting Edge.* Philadelphia: Temple University Press, 1995.

Devine, Philip E. *Human Diversity and the Culture Wars: A Philosophical Perspective on Contemporary Cultural Conflict.* Westport, CT: Praeger Publishers, 1996.

Dill, Bonnie Thornton. "Fictive Kin, Paper Sons, and *Compadrazgo:* Women of Color and the Struggle for Family Survival." In *Women of Color in U.S. Society,* ed. Maxine Baca Zinn and Bonnie Thornton Dill, 149–179.

Dinnerstein, Leonard, Roger L. Nichols, and David M. Reimers, eds. *Natives and Strangers: A Multicultural History of Americans.* Rev. ed. Oxford: Oxford University Press, 1996.

Domínguez, Virginia. *White by Definition: Social Classification in Creole Louisiana.* New Brunswick, NJ: Rutgers University Press, 1986.

Dooling, D. M., and Paul Jordan-Smith, eds. *I Become Part of It: Sacred Dimensions in Native American Life.* New York: Parabola Books, 1989.

D'Souza, Dinesh. *The End of Racism.* New York: Free Press, 1995.

Du Bois, W. E. B. *The Souls of Black Folk.* 1903. Reprint, New York: Penguin Books, 1989.

Dukes, Richard L., and Ruben Martinez. "The Impact of Ethgender Among Adolescents." *Adolescence* 29, no. 113 (Spring 1994): 105–115.

Ellison, Ralph. *Invisible Man.* New York: Random House, 1952.

Erdrich, Louise. *Love Medicine.* New York: Harper Collins, 1993.

Erikson, Erik. *Identity and the Life Cycle.* New York: W. W. Norton, 1980.

Espiritu, Yen Le. *Asian American Panethnicity: Bridging Institutions and Identities.* Philadelpha: Temple University Press, 1992.

Ezorsky, Gertrude. *Racism and Justice.* Ithaca, NY: Cornell University Press, 1991.

Fanon, Franz. *Black Skin, White Masks.* New York: Grove Press, 1967.

Farrakhan, Louis. "Interview in *National Alliance* Newspaper." In *Independent Black Leadership in America,* ed. William Pleasant, 7–53. New York: Castillo International Publications, 1990.

Fernández, Carlos. "La Raza and the Melting Pot." In *Racially Mixed People in America,* ed. Maria P. P. Root.

Fernández, Carlos A. "Testimony of the Association of MultiEthnic Americans." In *American Mixed Race,* ed. Naomi Zack, 126–143.

Finley, M. I. *Ancient Slavery and Modern Ideology.* New York: Pelican, 1983.

Fish, Stanley. "There's No Such Thing as Free Speech and It's a Good Thing." In *Today's Moral Issues: Classic and Contemporary Perspectives,* ed. Daniel Bonevac, 126–134. Mountainview, CA: Mayfield, 1996.

Flexner, Eleanor. *A Century of Struggle.* New York: Atheneum, 1974.

Fogelin, Robert J. *Understanding Arguments.* New York: Harcourt Brace Jovanovich, 1978.

Forbes, Jack D. *Black Africans and Native Americans: Color, Race and Caste in the Evolution of Red-Black Peoples.* London: Blackwell, 1988.

Foxworthy, Jeff. *Red Ain't Dead.* Atlanta: Longstreet Press, 1991.

Frankenberg, Ruth. *Displacing Whiteness: Essays in Social and Cultural Criticism.* Durham, NC: Duke University Press, 1997.

Frazier, Gregory W. *Urban Indians: Drums from the Cities.* Denver: Arrowstar Publishing, 1993.

Freire, Paulo. *Pedagogy of the Oppressed.* Trans. Myra Bergman Ramos. New York: Continuum, 1990.

Freydberg, Bridget A. "Sapphires, Spitfires, Sluts and Superbitches: Aframericans and Latinas in Contemporary American Film." In *Black Women in America,* ed. Kim Marie Vaz, 206–221.

Frye, Marilyn. "White Woman Feminist." In *Overcoming Sexism and Racism,* ed. Linda Bell and David Blumenfeld, 113–134.

Funderburg, L. *Black, White, Other: Biracial Americans Talk About Race and Identity.* New York: William Morrow, 1994.

Garcia, J. L. A. "Racism as a Model for Understanding Sexism." In *RACE/SEX,* ed. Naomi Zack, 45–60.

Geiger, Shirley M. "African-American Single Mothers: Public Perceptions and Public Policies." In *Black Women in America,* ed. Kim Marie Vaz, 244–260.

Giddings, Paula. *When and Where I Enter: The Impact of Black Women on Race and Sex in America.* New York: Bantam, 1984.

Gilman, Sander L. *Difference and Pathology: Stereotypes of Sexuality, Race and Madness.* Ithaca, NY: Cornell University Press, 1985.

Gilroy, Paul. *The Black Atlantic: Modernity and Double Consciousness.* Cambridge, MA: Harvard University Press, 1993.

Glazer, Nathan. "Individual Rights against Group Rights." In *The Rights of Minority Cultures,* ed. Will Kymlicka, 123–138.

Goffman, Irving. *The Presentation of Self in Everyday Life.* New York: Doubleday, 1959.

Goldberg, David Theo. *Racist Culture: Philosophy and the Politics of Meaning.* Cambridge, MA: Blackwell, 1993.

———. "Made in the USA." In *American Mixed Race,* ed. Naomi Zack, 237–256.

———, ed. *Anatomy of Racism.* Minneapolis: University of Minnesota Press, 1990.

———, ed. *Multiculturalism: A Critical Reader.* Oxford: Blackwell Publishers, 1994.

Goldberg, David, and Michael Krausz, eds. *Jewish Identity.* Philadelphia: Temple University Press, 1993.

Gordon, Lewis R. *Bad Faith and Antiblack Racism.* Atlantic Highlands, NJ: Humanities Press, 1995.

———. *Fanon and the Crisis of European Man: An Essay on Philosophy and the Human Sciences.* New York and London: Routledge, 1995.

———. "Race, Sex and Matrices of Desire in an Antiblack World." In *RACE/SEX,* ed. Naomi Zack, 117–132.

———, ed. *Existence in Black: An Anthology of Existentialist Black Philosophy.* New York: Routledge, 1997.

Gordon, Milton M. *Assimilation in American Life.* New York: Oxford University Press, 1964.

Gould, Stephen Jay. *The Mismeasure of Man.* New York: W. W. Norton, 1981.

Graham, Richard, ed. *The Idea of Race in Latin America, 1870–1940.* Austin: University of Texas Press, 1990.

Graham, Susan R. "Grassroots Advocacy." In *American Mixed Race*, ed. Naomi Zack, 185–190.

Grant, Joanne. *Black Protest: History, Documents and Analyses, 1619–Present.* New York: Ballantine Books, 1968.

Greene, B. A. "What Has Gone Before: The Legacy of Racism and Sexism in the Lives of Black Mothers and Daughters." In *Diversity and Complexity in Feminist Therapy,* ed. L. S. Brown and M. P. P. Root. New York: Haworth Press, 1990.

Gwaltney, John Langston. *Drylongso: A Self-Portrait of Black America.* New York: Vintage Books, 1980.

Hacker, Andrew. "Goodbye to Affirmative Action?" *New York Review of Books,* 11 July 1996, 21–26.

Hare, Nathan, and Julia Hare. *The Endangered Black Family.* San Francisco: Black Think Tank, 1984.

Hamilton, Cynthia. "Women, Home and Community: The Struggle in an Urban Environment." In *Living with Contradictions,* ed. Alison M. Jagger, 676–679.

Harmon, Alexandra. "When is An Indian Not an Indian? 'Friends of the Indian' and the Problem of Indian Identity." *Journal of Ethnic Studies* 18, no. 2 (1991): 95–123.

Harris, Leonard. "Honor: Emasculation and Empowerment." In *Rethinking Masculinity: Philosophical Explorations in Light of Feminism,* ed. Larry May and Robert A. Strikwerda, 191–208. Lanham, MD: Rowman and Littlefield, 1992.

———, ed. *Philosophy Born of Struggle: Anthology of Afro-American Philosophy since 1917.* Dubuque: Kendall/Hunt, 1983.

———, ed. *The Philosophy of Alain Locke.* Philadelphia: Temple University Press, 1989.

Harris, Virginia R. "Prison of Color." In *Racism in the Lives of Women,* ed. Jeanne Adleman and Gloria Enguídanos, 75–84. New York: Haworth, 1995.

Hawley, John C., ed. *Cross-Addressing: Resistance Literature and Cultural Borders.* Albany: State University of New York Press, 1997.

Hernton, Calvin. *Sex and Racism in America.* New York: Grove Press, 1965.

Hershel, Helena Jia. "Therapeutic Perspectives on Biracial Formation and Internalized Oppression." In *American Mixed Race,* ed. Naomi Zack, 169–184.

———. "The Influence of Gender and Race Status on Self-Esteem During Childhood and Adolescence." In *RACE/SEX,* ed. Naomi Zack, 109–116.

Hine, Darlene Clark. *Black Women in America: An Historical Encyclopedia.* 2 vols. Brooklyn, NY: Carlson, 1993.

Hines, P., and L. Berg-Cross. "Racial Differences in Global Self-Esteem." *Journal of Social Psychology* 113 (1981): 271–281.

Holmstrom, Nancy. "Do Women Have a Distinct Nature?" In *Women and Values: Readings in Recent Feminist Philosophy,* ed. Marjorie Pearsall. Belmont, CA: Wadsworth, 1986. [Reprinted from *Philosophical Forum* 14, no. 1 (Fall 1982): 25–42.]

———. "Race, Gender and Human Nature." In *RACE/SEX,* ed. Naomi Zack, 95–108.

Hong, Maria. *Growing Up Asian American: An Anthology.* New York: W. Morrow, 1993.

Hook, Sidney. *From Hegel to Marx.* Ann Arbor: University of Michigan, 1962.

hooks, bell. *Ain't I a Woman: Black Women and Feminism.* Boston: South End Press, 1981.

———. *Feminist Theory: From Margin to Center.* Boston: South End Press, 1984.

———. "Sisterhood: Political Solidarity between Women." In *Feminist Philosophies,* ed. Janet Kourany, James Sterba, and Rosemarie Tong. Englewood Cliffs, NJ: Prentice-Hall, 1992.

Horne, Gerald. "On the Criminalization of a Race." *Political Affairs* 73, no. 2 (February 1994): 26–30.

Horsman, Reginald. *Race and Manifest Destiny.* Cambridge, MA: Harvard University Press, 1981.

Hossfeld, Karen. "Hiring Immigrant Women: Silicon Valley's 'Simple Formula'." In *Women of Color in U.S. Society,* ed. Maxine Baca Zinn and Bonnie Thornton Dill , 65–94.

Hull, Gloria T. et al., eds. *All the Women are White, all the Blacks Are Men, But Some of Us Are Brave: Black Women's Studies.* New York: Feminist Press, 1982.

Ignatiev, Noel. *How the Irish Became White: Irish-Americans and African-Americans in 19th Century Philadelphia.* New York: Verso, 1995.

Ignatiev, Noel, and John Garvey, eds. *Race Traitor.* New York: Routledge, 1996.

Illinois Advisory Committee to the United States Commission on Civil Rights. *Civil Rights Issues Facing Asian Americans in Metropolitan Chicago.* Chicago: U.S. Commission on Civil Rights, 1995.

Jagger, Alison M., ed. *Living With Contradictions: Controversies in Feminist Social Ethics.* Boulder, CO: Westview Press, 1994.

Jaimes, M. Annette. "Some Kind of Indian." In *American Mixed Race,* ed. Naomi Zack, 133–154.

———, ed. *The State of Native America.* Boston: South End Press, 1992.

Jones, L. *Bulletproof Diva: Tales of Race, Sex, and Hair.* New York: Doubleday, 1994.

Jones, Maldwyn Allen. *American Immigration.* Chicago: University of Chicago Press, 1960.

Kang, Connie K. *Home Was the Land of Morning Calm: A Saga of A Korean American Family.* Reading, MA: Addison-Wesley, 1995.

Kellough, J. Edward. "Affirmative Action in Government Employment." *The Annals* 523 (September 1992): 117–130.

Kerner Report on Civil Disorders, Supplemental Studies for the National Advisory Commission on Civil Disorders. New York: Praeger, 1968. (See also, Assembly on The Kerner Report Revisited, Monticello, IL. 1970; *The Kerner Report Revisited.* Urbana, IL: Institute of Government and Public Affairs, University of Illinois, 1970.)

Kibria, Nazli. "Migration and Vietnamese American Women: Remaking Ethnicity." In *Women of Color in U.S. Society,* ed. Maxine Baca Zinn and Bonnie Thornton Dill, 247–264.

Kingston, Maxine Hong. *The Woman Warrior.* New York: Vintage, 1989.

Kovel, Joel. *White Racism: A Psychohistory.* London: Free Association, 1988.

Krupat, Arnold, ed. *Native American Autobiography: An Anthology.* Madison: University of Wisconsin Press, 1994.

Kuhl, Stefan. *The Nazi Connection: Eugenics, American Racism, and German National Socialism.* New York: Oxford University Press, 1994.

Kuhn, Thomas S. *The Structure of Scientific Revolutions.* Chicago: University of Chicago Press, 1970.

Kuper, Leo, ed. *Race, Science and Society.* New York: Columbia University Press, 1965.

Kymlicka, Will, ed. *The Rights of Minority Cultures.* Oxford: Oxford University Press, 1995.

Lang, Berel. *Act and Idea in the Nazi Genocide.* Chicago: University of Chicago Press, 1990.

———. "Metaphysical Racism." In *RACE/SEX,* ed. Naomi Zack, 17–28.

Laquer, Thomas. *Making Sex: Body and Gender from the Greeks to Freud.* Cambridge, MA: Harvard University Press, 1990.

Lawrence, Cecile Ann. "Racelessness." In *American Mixed Race,* ed. Naomi Zack, 299–307.

Lawson, Bill E., ed. *The Underclass Question.* Philadelphia: Temple University Press, 1992.

Leong, Russell. *Asian American Sexualities: Dimensions of the Gay and Lesbian Experience.* New York: Routledge, 1996.

Lesley, Craig, ed. *Talking Leaves: Contemporary Native American Short Stories.* New York: Dell, 1991.

Levine, Lawrence W. *Highbrow/Lowbrow: The Emergence of Cultural Hierarchy in America.* Cambridge, MA: Harvard University Press, 1988.

Lewontin, Richard C., Steven Rose, and Leon J. Kamin. *Not in Our Genes.* New York: Pantheon Books, 1984.

Ling, Amy. *Between Worlds: Women Writers of Chinese Ancestry.* New York: Pergammon Press, 1990.

Locke, John. "Some Thoughts Concerning Education." In *The Educational Writings of John Locke,* ed. James A. Axtell. Cambridge, MA: Cambridge University Press, 1968.

————. *Two Treatises of Government,* ed. Peter Laslett. Cambridge, MA: Cambridge University Press, 1991.

Lorde, Audre. *Sister Outsider.* Trumansburg, NY: Crossing Press, 1984.

————. "The Uses of Anger: Women Responding to Racism." In *Gender Basics,* ed. Anne Minas, 39–44.

Lott, Tommy L., ed. *Subjugation and Bondage: Critical Essays on Slavery and Social Philosophy.* Lanham, MD: Rowman and Littlefield, 1998.

Loury, Glenn. "Self-Censorship in Public Discourse." In *One By One From the Inside Out,* ed. Glenn Loury. New York: Free Press, 1995.

Lyden, Fremont J., and Lyman H. Legters, eds. *Native Americans and Public Policy.* Pittsburgh: University of Pittsburgh Press, 1992.

Macdonald, Andrew. *The Turner Diaries.* Hillsboro, VA: National Vanguard Books, 1978.

Machetti, Gina. *Romance and 'The Yellow Peril': Race, Sex and Discoursive Strategies in Hollywood Fiction.* Chicago: University of Chicago Press, 1993.

MacPherson, C. B. *The Political Theory of Possessive Individualism.* Oxford: Oxford University Press, 1970.

Malcolm X. *The Autobiography of Malcolm X* (as told to Alex Haley). New York: Ballantine, 1973.

Martin, Waldo E., Jr. *The Mind of Frederick Douglass.* Chapel Hill, NC: University of North Carolina Press, 1984.

Martinez, Ruben, and Richard L. Dukes. "Ethnic and Gender Differences in Self Esteem." *Youth & Society* 22, no. 3 (March 1991): 318–338.

Marx, Karl, and Frederick Engels. "The Communist Manifesto." In *Karl Marx, Selected Writings,* ed. Lawrence H. Simon. Indianapolis: Hackett, 1994.

Matsuda, Mari, Charles R. Lawrence, and Kimberle Williams Crenshaw. *Words that Wound: Critical Race Theory, Assaultive Speech, and the First Amendment.* Boulder, CO: Westview Press, 1993.

Matthiessen, Peter. *Indian Country.* New York: Viking, 1992.

McBride, James. *The Color of Water: A Black Man's Tribute to His White Mother.* New York: Riverhead Books, 1996.

McClintock, Ann, Jose Esteban Muñoz, and Trish Rosen, eds. *Race and Queer Sexuality.* *Social Text* 3–4 (1997).

McCord, David, and William Cleveland. *Black and Red: The Historical Meeting of Africans and Native Americans.* Atlanta: Dreamkeeper Press, Inc., 1990.

McGary, Howard. "Alienation and the African-American Experience." In *African-American Perspectives and Philosophical Traditions,* ed. John P. Pittman, 282–296.

McIntosh, Peggy. "White Privilege and Male Privilege: A Personal Account of Coming to See Correspondences Through Work in Women's Studies." In *Gender Basics,* ed. Anne Minas, 30–38.

Means, Russell. "Same Old Song." In *Marxism and Native Americans,* ed. Ward Churchill, 19–33.

Mencke, John G. *Mulattoes and Race Mixture: American Attitudes and Images, 1865–1918.* Ann Arbor: University Microfilms Inc. Research Press, 1979.

Michaels, Walter Benn. *Our America: Nativism, Modernism, and Pluralism.* Durham, NC: Duke University Press, 1995.

Miles, Kevin Thomas. "Body Badges: Race and Sex." In *RACE/SEX,* ed. Naomi Zack, 133–144.

Mill, John Stuart. *On Liberty.* Indianapolis: Hackett, 1978.

Minas, Anne, ed. *Gender Basics.* Belmont, CA: Wadsworth, 1993.

Momaday, N. Scott. *House of Dawn.* New York: Harper and Row, 1968.

Montagu, Ashley. *Man's Most Dangerous Myth: The Fallacy of Race.* Cleveland: World, 1964.

———. *The Concept of Race.* London: Collier Books, 1969.

Moody-Adams, Michelle. "Race, Class, and the Social Construction of Self-Respect." In *African-American Perspectives and Philosophical Traditions,* ed. John P. Pittman, 251–266.

Morrison, Toni. *The Bluest Eye.* New York: Washington Square, 1970.

———, ed. *Race-ing Justice, En-gendering Power: Essays on Anita Hill, Clarence Thomas and the Construction of Social Reality.* New York: Pantheon Books, 1992.

Nabokov, Peter, ed. *Native American Testimony: A Chronicle of Indian-White Relations from Prophecy to the Present.* New York: Penguin Books, 1991.

Nelson, Hilde Lindemann. *Feminism and Families.* New York: Routledge, 1996.

Newton, Lisa H. "Reversed Discrimination as Unjustified." In *Living With Contradictions,* ed. Alison M. Jagger, 62–65.

Nicholson, Linda. *Gender and History.* New York: Columbia University Press, 1986.

———. "The Myth of the Traditional Family." In *Feminism and Families,* ed. Hilde Lindemann Nelson, 27–42.

Nobles, Wade W., and Goddard L. Lawford. *Understanding the Black Family.* Oakland, CA: The Institute for the Advanced Study of Black Family Life and Culture, 1984.

Noonan, Harold W. *Personal Identity.* London: Routledge, 1989.

Novick, Michael. *White Lies, White Power: The Fight Against White Supremacy and Reactionary Violence.* Monroe, ME: Common Courage, 1995.

Omi, Michael, and Howard Winant. *Racial Formation in the U.S. 1960–1980.* New York: Routledge & Kegan Paul, 1986.

Outlaw, Lucius T. *On Race and Philosophy.* New York: Routledge, 1996.

Pittman, John P. "Malcolm X: Masculinist Practice and Queer Theory." In *RACE/SEX,* ed. Naomi Zack, 205–217.

Pittman, John P., ed. *African-American Perspectives and Philosophical Traditions.* New York: Routledge, 1996.

Plato. *The Republic.* Trans. Desmond Lee. New York: Penguin, 1987.

Putnam, Emily James. *The Lady: Studies of Certain Significant Phases of Her History.* Chicago: University of Chicago Press, 1970.

Rauch, Jonathan. "The Humanitarian Threat." In *Today's Moral Issues: Classic and Contemporary Perspectives,* ed. Daniel Bonevac, 135–148. Mountainview, CA: Mayfield Publishing Co., 1995.

Riccucci, Norma M. "Merit, Equity, and Test Validity." *Administration and Society* 23, no. 1 (May 1991): 74–93.

Ridgeway, James. *Blood in the Face.* New York: Thundermouth Press, 1990.

Riggs, Marlon. "Sexuality, Television, and Death: A Black Gay Dialogue on Malcolm X." In *Malcolm X: In Our Own Image,* ed. Joe Wood. New York: Doubleday, 1992.

Rodriguez, Richard. *Hunger of Memory: The Education of Richard Rodriguez.* Boston: D. R. Godine, 1981.

Roediger, David R. *The Wages of Whiteness: Race and the Making of the American Working Class.* London: Verso, 1992.

Root, M. P. P. "A Bill of Rights for Racially Mixed People." In *The Multiracial Experience,* ed. Root, 3–14.

———. "The Multiracial Contribution to the Psychological Browning of America." In *American Mixed Race,* ed. Naomi Zack, 231–236.

———, ed. *Racially Mixed People in America.* Newbury Park, CA: Sage, 1993.

———, ed. *The Multiracial Experience: Racial Borders as the New Frontier.* Thousand Oaks, CA: Sage Publications, 1996.

Roth, Henry. *Call It Sleep.* New York: Cooper Square, 1970.

Russell, Kathy, Midge Wilson, and Ronald Hall. *The Color Complex: The Politics of Skin Color Among African Americans.* New York: Harcourt Brace Jovanovich, 1992.

Said, Edward. *Orientalism.* New York: Random House, 1978.

Sartre, Jean-Paul. *Anti-Semite and Jew.* New York: Schocken Books, 1948.

Sartwell, Crispin. *Act Like You Know: African-American Autobiograpy and White Identity.* Chicago: University of Chicago Press, 1998.

Scales-Trent, Judy. *Notes of a White Black Woman.* University Park, PA: Pennsylvania State University Press, 1995.

Scheik, William J. *The Half-Blood: A Cultural Symbol in 19th-Century American Fiction.* Lexington, KY: University Press of Kentucky, 1979.

Schusky, Ernest L. *The Right to be Indian.* San Francisco: American Indian Educational Publishers, 1970.

Schutte, Ofelia. *Cultural Identity and Social Liberation in Latin American Thought.* Albany: State University of New York Press, 1993.

Shrage, Laurie. *Moral Dilemmas of Feminism: Prostitution, Adultery, and Abortion.* New York: Routledge, 1994.

———. "Ethnic Transgressions: Confessions of an Assimilated Jew." In *American Mixed Race,* ed. Naomi Zack, 287–296.

———. "Passing Beyond the Other Race or Sex." In *RACE/SEX,* ed. Naomi Zack, 183–190.

Sidel, Ruth. *Women and Children Last: The Plight of Poor Women in Affluent America.* New York: Penguin Books, 1992.

Singer, L. "Ethnogenesis and Negro-Americans Today." *Social Research* 29, no. 4 (Winter 1962): 419–432.

Sleeter, C. E., ed. *Empowerment through Multicultural Education.* Albany: State University of New York Press, 1991.

Smith, Adam. *Wealth of Nations: An Inquiry into the nature and causes of the wealth of nations.* 2 vols. Ed. H. H. Cambell, A. S. Skinner, and W. B. Todd. Oxford: Clarendon Press, 1976.

Sowell, Thomas. *The Economics and Politics of Race: An International Perspective.* New York: William Morrow, 1983.

———. *Civil Rights: Rhetoric or Reality?* New York: William Morrow, 1984.

Spickard, Paul. *Mixed Blood: Intermarriage and Ethnic Identity in Twentieth Century America.* Madison: University of Wisconsin Press, 1989.

Squire-Hakey, Mariella. "Yankee Imperialism and Imperialist Nostalgia." In *American Mixed Race,* ed. Naomi Zack, 221–229.

Stanton, William. *The Leopard's Spots: Scientific Attitudes Toward Race in America, 1819–59.* Chicago: University of Chicago Press, 1960.

Statistical Record of Asian Americans. Detroit, MI: Gale Research, Inc. 1993.

Statistical Record of Black Americans. Detroit, MI: Gale Research, Inc. 1990.

Statistical Record of Native North Americans. Detroit, MI: Gale Research, Inc. 1993.

Steinberg, Steven. *The Ethnic Myth.* Boston: Beacon Press, 1989.

Stepan, Nancy Leys. *The Idea of Race in Science: Great Britain, 1800–1950.* London: Archon Books, 1982.

———. "Race and Gender: The Role of Analogy in Science." In *Anatomy of Racism,* ed. David Theo Goldberg, 38–57.

Sterba, James P. *Contemporary Social and Political Philosophy*. Belmont, CA: Wadsworth, 1995.

———. "Racism and Sexism: The Common Ground." In *RACE/SEX*, ed. Naomi Zack, 61–74.

Stevens, Evelyn P. "Marianismo: The Other Face of Machismo in Latin America." In *Gender Basics*, ed. Anne Minas, 483–490.

Stone, Lawrence. *The Family, Sex and Marriage in England, 1500–1800*. New York: Harper and Row, 1979.

Stowe, David. "*Un*colored People: The Rise of Whiteness Studies." *Lingua Franca* (Sept/Oct 1996): 68–77.

Streeter, Caroline A. "Ambiguous Bodies: Locating Black/White Women in Cultural Representations." In *The Multiracial Experience*, ed. Maria P. P. Root, 305–322.

Stuart, I., and L. Abt, eds. *Interracial Marriage: Expectations and Realities*. New York: Grossman Publishers, 1973.

Sundquist, Åsebrit. *Pocahontas & Co.: The Fictional American Indian Woman in Nineteenth-Century Literature: A Study of Method*. Atlantic Highlands, NJ: Humanities Press International, 1987.

Takaki, Ronald. *Strangers from a Different Shore: A History of Asian Americans*. New York: Penguin Books, 1989.

Tedlock, Dennis, and Barbara Tedlock, eds. *Teachings from the American Earth*. New York: Liveright, 1975.

Tenzer, L. R. *A Completely New Look at Interracial Sexuality: Public Opinion and Select Commentaries*. Manahawkin, NJ: Scholar's Publishing House, 1990.

Thernstrom, Stephen, ed. *Harvard Encyclopedia of American Ethnic Groups*. Cambridge, MA: Belknap Press of Harvard University Press, 1980.

Thomas, Laurence. "Sexism and Racism: Some Conceptual Differences." *Ethics* 90 (1980): 239–250.

———. "Moral Flourishing in an Unjust World." *Journal of Moral Education* 22, no. 2 (1993): 83–96.

———. "Moral Deference." In *African-American Perspectives and Philosophical Traditions*, ed. John P. Pittman, 233–250.

Thomas, Laurence Mordekhai. *Vessels of Evil*. Philadelphia: Temple University Press, 1993.

Thomson, Judith Jarvis. *The Realm of Rights*. Cambridge, MA: Harvard University Press, 1990.

Thornton, Russell. *American Indian Holocaust Survival: A Population History Since 1492*. Norman, OK: University of Oklahoma Press, 1987.

Twain, Mark. *The Tragedy of Pudd'nhead Wilson*. New York: Norton, 1980.

United Nations Charter: The Universal Declaration of Human Rights, reprinted in *Vice and Virtue in Everyday Life*, ed. Christina Sommers and Fred Sommers, 203–209. Fort Worth, TX: Harcourt Brace, 1993.

U.S. Bureau of the Census. *Characteristics of the Population*. Vol. 1, Part 1, Sections 1 and 2. Washington, DC: Government Printing Office, 1970.

U.S. Bureau of the Census. *Census of Population: General Population Characteristics—United States*. Vol. 1990 CP-1-1. Washington, DC: Government Printing Office, 1990.

Vaz, Kim Marie, ed., *Black Women in America*. Thousand Oaks, CA: Sage, 1995.

Wacker, R. Fred. *Ethnicity, Pluralism and Race*. Westwood, CT: Greenwood, 1983.

Walker, Alice. *In Search of Our Mothers' Gardens*. New York: Harcourt Brace Jovanovich, 1983.

Walzer, Michael. "Pluralism: A Political Perspective." In *The Rights of Minority Cultures*, ed. Will Kymlicka, 139–154.

Webster, Yehudi O. *The Racialization of America*. New York: St. Martin's Press, 1992.

Weisner, Merry E. *Women and Gender in Early Modern Europe.* Cambridge, MA: Cambridge University Press, 1993.

West, Cornel. *Race Matters.* Boston: Beacon Press, 1993.

Westra, Laura, and Peter S. Wenz, eds. *Faces of Environmental Racism.* Lanham, MD: Rowman and Littlefield, 1995.

Williams, Patricia. *The Alchemy of Race and Rights.* Cambridge, MA: Harvard University Press, 1991.

———. *The Rooster's Egg: On the Persistence of Prejudice.* Cambridge, MA: Harvard University Press, 1995.

Williamson, Joel. *New People.* New York: Free Press, 1980.

Willie, C. V. *Oreo: Race and Marginal Men and Women.* Wakefield, MA: Parameter Press, 1975.

Wilson, Terry P. "Blood Quantum: Native American Mixed Bloods." In *Racially Mixed People in America,* ed. Maria P. P. Root, 108–125.

Wilson, William Julius. *The Truly Disadvantaged.* Chicago: University of Chicago Press, 1987.

———. "Studying Inner-City Social Dislocations: The Challenge of Public Agenda Research." *American Sociological Review* 56 (February 1991): 10.

Wolfman, Brunetta. "Color Fades Over Time." In *American Mixed Race,* ed. Naomi Zack, 13–24.

Wray, Matt, and Annalee Newitz, eds. *White Trash: Race and Class.* New York: Routledge, 1997.

Wright, Richard. *The Outsider.* New York: Harper and Row, 1953.

———. *Black Power: A Record of Reactions in a Land of Pathos.* New York: Harper and Brothers, 1954.

Young, Iris Marion. *Justice and the Politics of Difference.* Princeton, NJ: Princeton University Press, 1990.

Zack, Naomi. *Race and Mixed Race.* Philadelphia: Temple University Press, 1993.

———. "Life After Race." In *American Mixed Race,* ed. idem, 297–308.

———. "Mixed Black and White Race and Public Policy," *Hypatia* (Feminist Ethics and Social Policy, Part I) Vol. 10 No. 1, Winter 1995, pp. 120–132.

———. *Bachelors of Science: Seventeenth Century Identity, Then and Now.* Philadelphia: Temple University Press, 1996.

———. " 'The Family' and Radical Family Theory." In *Feminism and Families,* ed. Hilde Lindemann Nelson, 43–53.

———. "On Being and Not-Being Black and Jewish." In *The Multiracial Experience,* ed. Maria P. P. Root, 140–151.

———. "The American Sexualization of Race" and "Race and Philosophic Meaning." In *RACE/SEX,* ed. idem, 29–44 and 145–156.

———, ed. *American Mixed Race: The Culture of Microdiversity.* Lanham, MD: Rowman and Littlefield, 1995.

———, ed. *RACE/SEX: Their Sameness, Difference and Interplay.* New York: Routledge, 1997.

Zinn, Maxine Baca, and Bonnie Thornton Dill, eds. *Women of Color in U.S. Society.* Philadelphia: Temple University Press, 1994.

INDEX

Note: terms that are in boldface in text and defined in glossary are followed by **g.** Full citations of books listed here and in Recommended Reading sections are in the Bibliography.